A PALI PRIMER

A PALI PRIMER

MAUNG TIN

GYAN

Published by

GYAN

Gyan Publishing House
5, Ansari Road
Daryaganj, New Delhi-110002
Phone: 011-47034999, 9811692060
E-mail: books@gyanbooks.com

Distribution Network
gyanbooks.com
India, USA, Canada, UK, Australia, France

ISBN : 978-81-212-4487-9 (PB)
First Published, Rangoon, 1914

2nd Impression 2020

Printed at: Gyan Press, Delhi.

A Pali Primer
Author: Maung Tin

A
PĀLI PRIMER

BY

MAUNG TIN, M.A.,

Professor of Pali, Rangoon College.

RANGOON:

PRINTED AT THE BRITISH BURMA PRESS.

1914.

PREFACE.

Within the compass of this little book, I have tried to give as much of Pali grammar with exercise as should be sufficient for beginners. My intention has been not to write a complete treatise on grammar in all its ramifications but to present its salient points in the simplest garb possible. I have thus thought it to my purpose to skip over many things which would only puzzle the beginner and which should find a place only in a complete grammatical treatise. For it is my belief that it is a sounder plan to restrict the beginner to the important features of grammar than to make him stray over a wider field with less profit.

I hope therefore that this little book will be of some use to beginners. If properly studied it should furnish a good step towards surmounting the intricacies of higher grammar. As a matter of fact, I have aimed at placing it mid-way between Gray's second Pali Course (a very good book whose only fault is its narrow limits) and Duroiselle's Pali Grammar which is too good for beginners. I have derived much profit from both these books.

M. T.

RANGOON
27th April 1914.

CONTENTS.

ERRATA.

Page.	*line.*	*for*	*read*
12	25	pachā	pacchā
18	20	aṭṭhiḥi	aṭṭhihi
19	6	cakkhumiṁ	cakkhusmiṁ
19	10	Ayu	Āyu
23	22	mayaṁ	te
25	25	pancantī	pacantī
29	8	that	this
33	2	*kim*	*kiṁ*
33	4 (*fr. bottom*)	karaṇaṁ	kāraṇaṁ
34	2 (*fr. bottom*)	*ummattka*	*ummattaka*
37	4	√ha	√hā
39	6	tīni	tīṇi
41	22	guniṭṭha	guṇiṭṭha
43	9	pita āgacchāyya	pitā āgaccheyya
44	*last line*	khādanīyam	khādanīyaṁ
48	*last line*	si	āsi
49	6 (*fr. bottom*)	hotu	hotū
51	9 (*fr. bottom*)	rāja	rājā
62	16	Aṭṭhasi	Aṭṭhāsi
62	17	Atthạsi	Aṭṭhāsi
71	*last but one*	Sakka	Sakko
73	1	hitaya	hitāya
73	7	main	maṁ

Inrtoductory Lessons.

The Pali alphabet consists of 41 letters—8 vowels and 33 consonants.

The eight vowels are :—

a	pronounced as	*a*	in	*hart.*
ā	"	*a*	"	*father.*
i	"	*i*	"	*pin.*
ī	"	*ee*	"	*keen.*
u	"	*u*	"	*bull.*
ū	"	*oo*	"	*boon.*
e	"	*ay*	"	*bay.*
o	"	*o*	"	*tone.*

Of these three are short, *viz.* a, i, u and the rest are long.

The thirty-three consonants are :—

kind.	THE 25 LETTERS OF THE FIVE GROUPS.					Others.	
	Hard.	Hard Aspirate.	Soft.	Soft Aspirate.	Nasal.		
Group I. Gutturals or *Throat letters.*	k	kh	g	gh	ṅ		
Group II. Palatals or *Front-palate letters.*	c	ch	j	jh	ñ	y	s
Group III. Cerebrals or *Back-palate letters.*	ṭ	ṭh	ḍ	ḍh	ṇ	r	ḷ
Group IV. Dentals or *Tooth letters.*	t	th	d	dh	n	l	
Group V. Labials or *Lip letters.*	p	ph	b	bh	m	v	

and h and ṁ.

Properly speaking, these consonants cannot be sounded without the help of a vowel So, in naming them, the vowel *a* is sounded after each, *e.g.*, *k* is sounded as *ka* *p* as *pa* and so on. When any other vowel is attached to them, they take the sound of that vowel. Thus *ku, ki, ud, in,* etc.

N.B.—*c* is pronounced like *ch* in *church*, *j* as in *jar*, *ñ* like *ny* in *banyan*; *ṁ* is called *niggahita* and is sounded like *ng* in *king* with a slight suppression of the breath.

Lesson I.

DECLENSION OF MASCULINE NOUNS IN A.

The way in which case-endings are added to the *stem* or the crude part of a noun is called declension, *e.g.* Putta, son, is declined as follows :

Singular.

Nom.	Putt*o*	... the son.
Gen.	Putta*ssa*	... the son's, of the son.
Dat.	Putta*ssa*, Putt*āya*	to *or* for the son.
Acc.	Putta*ṁ*	... the son.
Ins.	Putt*ena*	... by *or* through the son.
Abl.	Putt*ā*, Putta*smā*, Putta*mhā*, Put-ta*to*	from the son.
Loc.	Putt*e*, Putta*smiṁ*, Putta*mhi*	in *or* on the son.
Voc.	Putta	... O son !

Plural.

Nom.	Putt*ā*	... the sons.
Gen. Dat.	Putt*ānaṁ*	... the sons', of, to *or* for the sons.

Acc.	Putt*e*	... the sons.
Ins. Abl.	Putt*ehi*, Putt*ebhi*	by, through *or* from the sons.
Loc.	Putt*esu*	... in *or* on the sons.
Voc.	Putt*ā*	... O sons!

The case-endings are shown by the italicised letters. The vowel *a* which denotes the stem is dropped in contact with those endings beginning with a vowel, *e.g.*, Putta+o =putto. The true ending for the loc. sing. is *i*, which in contact with *a* becomes *e*, *i.e* putta+i= putte. Similarly in the ins. sing. putta+ina=puttena.

The student will understand these changes better when he learns sandhi. He might now be content to remember the case-endings as they stand. Note also that before *hi*, *bhi* and *su* the vowel *a* is changed to *e*.

Exercise:—Decline like Putta, the following nouns:— sīha, lion; miga, deer; amacca, minister; sadda, sound; ludda, hunter; suriya, sun.

Lesson II.

Pali verbs are divided into seven classes according to the seven ways of attaching the conjugational signs to the root.

FIRST CONJUGATION (FIRST DIVISION).

The sign of the first conjugation is *a*, which is added to the root in four ways. The first consists in adding *a* directly to the root, which ends in a consonant. The root thus becomes the base, *e.g.*

√pac + a = paca.

To the base *paca* add the personal endings or tense terminations and the verb is obtained. Thus

Present Tense, Active Voice.

Persons.	*Singular.*	*Plural*
1st	Ahaṁ pacā*mi*, I cook.	Mayaṁ pacā*ma*, we cook.
2nd	Tvaṁ paca*si*, thou cookest.	Tumhe paca*tha*, you cook.
3rd	So, sā, taṁ paca*ti*, he, she, it cooks.	Te, ta, tāni paca*nti*, they cook.

Note that the vowel is lengthened before *mi* and *ma*.

Exercise.—Conjugate (like √ pac) √ rakkh, to guard; √ vadh, to kill; √ yāc, to request; √ pucch, to question; √ labh, to get; √ mar, to die.

Translate into English:—1. Sihā maranti. 2. Luddā mige vadhanti. 3. Tvaṁ amacce pucchasi.

Translate into Pali:—1. The lion kills the deer. 2. They ask the ministers. 3. We get a lion.

Lesson III.

FIRST CONJUGATION (Second division).

The root of this division of verbs ends in a long vowel, mostly *ā* and the tense terminations are added directly, *e.g.* √ yā, to go—yāmi, I go, etc., etc.

Exercise: (like √ yā) √ vā, to blow; √ brū, to say; √ khyā, to tell (with prefix ā).

Declension of feminine nouns in ā.

kaññā—a girl.

	Singular.	*Plural.*
Nom	Kaññā	Kaññā, Kaññāyo
Gen. Dat.	Kaññāya.	Kaññānaṁ.

Acc.	Kaññaṁ·	Kaññā, Kaññāyo.
Ins. Abl.	Kaññāya.	Kaññāhi, Kaññābhi.
Loc.	Kaññāya, Kaññāyaṁ:	Kaññāsu.
Voc.	Kañña, Kaññe.	Kaññā, Kaññāyo.

Note that *ya* is common to gen. dat. inst. abl. and loc.

Vocabulary of feminine nouns in ā:—nāvā, boat; bāhā, arm; jālā, flame; vācā, speech; vedanā, pain; chāyā, shadow.

Feminine suffixes: *ā* is a characteristic fem. sign. Another is *ī*, varied into nī, inī, ānī., *e.g.* sihī, lioness; bhikkhunī, nun; miginī, doe; mātulānī, aunt.

Translations:—1. Ahaṁ nāvāya yāmi. 2. Sihī vedanāya marati. 3. Luddā suriyassa chāyaṁ labhanti. 4. Tumhe vācaṁ brūtha.

1. The girl dies on the arm of the hunter. 2. They die in the shade of the boat. 3. The hunter goes through the flame. 4. She speaks the word.

Lesson IV.

FIRST CONJUGATION (THIRD DIVISION).

The root ends in i, ī, u or ū which, together with the conjugational sign *a*, are changed into *e* or *aya* and *o* or *ava*. (i, ī+a=e; u, ū+a=o) *e.g.*

√nī, to lead+a=ne or naya+ti=neti, nayati.
√ji, to conquer+a=je or jaya+ti=jeti, jayati.
√bhū, to be+a=bho or bhavati+ti=bhoti, bhavati.
√ku, to sing+a=kava+ti=kavati.

DECLENSION OF NEUTER NOUNS IN *A*.

This is exactly the same as the declension of mas. nouns in *a*, except in the nom. sing. which ends in *ṁ* and the nom. and voc. pl., which end in *āni*, the characteristic neuter plural sign., *e.g.* gharaṁ, a house; gharāni, houses, O houses!

Vocabulary of neuter nouns:—raṭṭha, country; sakaṭa, cart; osadha, medicine; hadaya, heart; cetiya, shrine; jīvita, life; rūpa, form; vajira, diamond; vāta, wind; mūla, root, price.

Translations:—1. Mayaṁ sakaṭena yāma. 2. Miginī vedanaṁ labhati. 3. Mātulānī cetiyassa chāyāyaṁ marati. 4. Luddassa bāhā kaññaṁ rakkhati.

1. The girl obtains the price of the diamond. 2. You ask the minister in the country. 3. We protect the kingdom of the girl from the sons. 4. The hunter conquers the kingdom.

Lesson V.

SANDHI.

The changes which occur when one word meets with another are regulated by the rules of sandhi, which may be divided into three kinds, *viz.*, vowel sandhi, mixed sandhi and niggahīta sandhi.

(*a*) Vowel sandhi occurs when a word *ending in a vowel*, meets a word *beginning with a vowel.*

(*b*) Mixed sandhi occurs when a word ending in a vowel meets a word *beginning with a consonant.*

(*c*) Niggahīta sandhi occurs when a word *ending in niggahita* meets a word beginning either with a vowel or a consonant.

Examples (*a*) yassa+idāni=yass' idāni (*a* being elided).
(*b*) vi+payutta=vippayutta (*p* being doubled).
(*c*) labheyyaṁ ahaṁ=labheyyâhaṁ (*ṁ* being elided).

More examples will be given in the course of the lessons. Sandhi is more easily learnt by observing its changes met with in the literature than from the rules of grammar. The student should, however, observe the following changes :—

(*a*) a, ā+i, ī=e, as ava+icca=avecca.
(*b*) a, ā+u, ū=o, as, na+upeti=nopeti.

The contrary change also holds good, *i.e.*

(*c*) i, ī+a, ā=e, as. nī+ati=neti.
(*d*) u, ū+a. ā=o, as bhū+ati=bhoti.

When two vowels of the same organ meet, the result is a long vowel; *i.e.*—

(*e*) a, ā+a,ā=ā, as na+ahosi=nâhosi.
(*f*) i, i+i, ı=ī, as demi+iti=demîti.
(*g*) u, ū+u, ū=ū, as madhu+udakaṁ=Madhûdakaṁ.

When vowels of different organs meet, one of them is elided·

e.g. (*h*) atha+eko=ath'eko (*final* vowel being elided).
(*i*) Ko+asi=ko'si (*initial* vowel being elided).

In such instances the general rule is that a, ā are elided before or after i, ī or u, ū and i, ī before or after u, ū. But the student must be prepared to meet with exceptional cases.

PERSONAL PRONOUNS.

Ahaṁ—I (First person).

	Singular.	*Plural.*
Nom.	ahaṁ	mayaṁ.
Gen. Dat.	me, mama, mayhaṁ	amhākaṁ.
Acc.	maṁ	amhe.
Ins., Abl.	me, mayā	amhehi, amhebhi.

Loc.	mayi	amhesu.

Note:—*no* may be used for all the cases of the plural, as, niyyāmako no hohi, be thou our captain (no=amhākaṁ)

Tvaṁ—thou (Second person).

	Singular.	*Plural.*
Nom.	tvaṁ.	tumhe.
Gen., Dat.	te tava, tuyhaṁ.	tumhākaṁ.
Acc.	taṁ	tumhe.
Ins. Abl.	te tayā	tumhehi, tumhebhi.
Loc.	tayi.	tumhesu.

Note:—*vo* may be used for all the cases of the plural, as, mātā vo pāpaṁ karoti—your mother commits sin (vo=tumhākaṁ); *no* and *vo* must not begin a sentence.

So—he (Third person, mas.)

	Singular.	*Plural.*
Nom.	so.	te.
Gen., Dat.	tassa.	tesaṁ.
Acc.	taṁ.	te.
Ins.	tena	} tehi, tebhi.
Abl.	tasmā, tamhā.	
Loc.	tasmiṁ, tamhi.	tesu.

Sā,—she (Third person, fem.)

	Singular.	*Plural.*
Nom.	sā.	tā, tāyo.
Gen., Dat.	tāya, tassā, tissā.	tāsaṁ.
Acc.	taṁ.	tā, tāyo.
Ins., Abl.	tāya.	tāhi, tābhi.
Loc.	tāya, tāyaṁ, tissāya, tissāyaṁ	tāsu.

Taṁ—it (Third person, neuter.)

	Singular.	*Plural.*
Nom.	taṁ.	tāni.
Gen., Dat.	tassa.	ṁtesa.

Acc.	taṁ.	tāni.
Ins.	tena,	tehi, tebhi.
Abl.	tasmā, tamhā.	
Loc.	tasmiṁ, tamhi.	tesu.

Vocabulary :—gacchati, goes ; nisidati, sits ; dhovati, washes ; khanati, digs ; nipajjati, lies down ; ovadati, admonishes.

Note :—(*a*) Verbs of motion govern the accusative, as, So raṭṭhaṁ gacchati—he goes to the country.

(*b*) Verbs of *asking* and *telling* govern two accusatives, as So dhammaṁ maṁ pucchati—he asks me about the Law.

Translations —1. Mama siho tassā migaṁ vadhati. 2. Sā tesaṁ bāhāyo dhovati. 3. Mayaṁ tassa Sakaṭassa chāyāyaṁ nipajjāma. 4. Sā tesaṁ kaññaṁ pañhaṁ (question, *mas.*) pucchati. 5. Amaccā bhattaṁ (*n.* food.) pacanti.

1. The girl sits on the minister's arm. 2. They dig for the root. 3. The son instiucts the girl in the shade of the shrine. 4. We go to the ministers' country in a cart. (*use the inst.*) 5. They lie down on the ground (mahı, f.)

Lesson VI.

FIRST CONJUGATION (FOURTH DIVISION).

Reduplication consists in the doubling of the first consonant of the root together with the following vowel, as, √dā, to give, becomes dadā by reduplication.

In this conjugation, the base is obtained by reduplicating the root.

The rules of reduplication are—

(*a*) a guttural is reduplicated by a palatal, as √gam to go—*ja*gam :

(*b*) *h* is replaced by *j*, as, √ha, to abandon—*ja*hā ;

(*c*) an unaspirate is used in the reduplicative syllable, as, √khan—*ca*khan ;

(*d*) *v* is replaced by *u*, as, √vas, to live—*u*vāsa ;

(*e*) a long vowel is shortened in the reduplicative syllable and generally—

a, ā becomes a, as, √dā—dadā.
i, ī „ i, as, √chid, to cut—ciccheda.
u, ū „ u (sometimes a), as, √bhū—babhuva.
i is sometimes changed to e in the reduplicated syllable as also u to o, as √chid—ciccheda and √budh, to know—bubodha.

AORIST TENSE.

	Singular.	*Plural.*
1.	paciṁ	pacimhā.
2.	paci	pacittha.
3.	paci	paciṁsu.

DECLENSION OF MASCULINE NOUNS IN i, ī.

Kapi - monkey.

	Singular.	*Plural.*
Nom.	kapi	kapi, kap*ayo*
Gen. Dat.	kapino, kap*issa*	kapīnaṁ.
Acc.	kapiṁ	kapī, kap*ayo*.
Ins.	kapinā	kapīhi.
Abl.	kapinā, kapismā, kapimhā.	kapīhi.
Loc.	kapimhi, kapismiṁ	kapīsu.
Voc.	Kapi	kapi, kap*ayo*.

Note *kapayo* in the pl.

Sakkhī—witness.

	Singular.	*Plural.*
Nom.	sakkhī	sakkhī, sakkh*ino*.

Gen. Dat.	sakkhino, sakkhissa	sakkhīnaṁ.
Acc.	sakkhiṁ, sakkhi*naṁ*	sakkhī, sakkhi*no*.
Ins.	sakkhinā ...	sakkhīhi.
Abl.	sakkhinā, sakkhismā, sakkhimhā ...	
Loc.	sakkhiṣmiṁ, sakkhimhi ...	sakkhīsu.
Voc.	sakkhi ...	sakkhī, sakkhi*no*.

Note the acc. sing. and nom. and acc. pl. forms. Sakkhi is also found in the nom. sing.

Nouns (like kapi);—aggi, fire; asani, thunderbolt; gahapati, householder; isi, saint; muni, sage; nidhi, treasure; sārathi, charioteer; rāsi, heap; maṇi, gem.

Nouns (like sakkhi):—hatthī, elephant; verī, enemy; seṭṭhī, banker; mantī, counsellor; kuṭṭhī, leper; pāpakārī, sinner.

Verbs of the First Conjugation:—carati √car, walks; daṁsati √daṁs, bites; dhāvati √dhāv, runs; disati √dis, sees; icchati √is, wishes, khādati √khād, eats; khipati √khip, throws; ramati √ram, plays, delights in; sikkhati √sikkh, learns, teaches.

Translations:—1. Gahapatayo osadhaṁ khādanti. 2. Mayaṁ vajiraṁ icchimhā. 3. Tāyo nidhīnaṁ rāsimhi nisīdiṁsu. 4 Sārathi raṭṭhena raṭṭhaṁ (from country to country) carati. 5. Mayaṁ kaññāya jīvitaṁ dadāma. 6. Te mama bhattaṁ khādiṁsu.

1. She threw the diamond on the shrine. 2. The enemies ran away in a cart (*ins.*) 3. I lay down in the boat. 4. They washed his body with water (udakaṁ). 5. My aunt desired fire. 6. They saw the leper in the shade of the shrine.

Lesson VII.

SECOND CONJUGATION.

Niggahita is inserted before the final consonant of the root, when the niggahīta is changed to the nasal of the group (one of the 5 groups) to which the final consonant belongs, *e.g.* √rudh, to check—rundha; √muc, to be free—muñca; √chid, to cut—chinda; √lip, to besmear—limpa; √bhuj, to eat—bhuñja; √pis, to grind—piṁsa.

IMPERATIVE.

	Singular.	*Plural.*
1.	pacāmi	pacāma
2.	pacāhi, paca	pacatha
3	pacatu	pacantu.

Note that the base itself is used for the second sing.

Prepositions.—Saha, saddhiṁ—"with", *vinā*—"without" are used with the instrumentive; *adhi*—" above " is used with the locative and *pati*—" against ", " for the sake of " is used with the accusative, as, puttena saha (or saddhiṁ) gacchati—he goes with the son. Vinā dosena bhāsati—he speaks without fault. Sakuṇo adhi pabbate palāyati—the bird flies over the mountain. Nadiṁ pati dhāvanti—they run against the river.

The following prepositions are construed with the genitive:—upari, above; heṭṭhā, under; purato, in front; pachā, pacchato, behind; antare, within; bāhire, outside; orato, on this side; dūre, dūrato, far; pāraṁ, pārato, beyond, on the other side; santike, samīpe, near, in the presence of; avidūre, not far away.

Translations:—1. Sā sakaṭassa upari nipajjati. 2. Mayaṁ nāvāya heṭṭhā vajiraṁ khipimhā. 3. Kaññāyo amaccassa purato nisidanti. 4. Mama pacchā cara. 5. So raṭṭhassa antare dhāvati. 6. Te samuddassa (m. ocean) pāraṁ vasiṁsu. 7. Mama puttena saddhiṁ gaccha.

1. Dig outside the kingdom. 2. Let them eat the medicine on this side of the mountain. 3. Sit far away from the girl. 4. They obtained treasure on this side of the ocean. 5. Sit thou near the banker's son. 6. Ask him a question. 7. Let the birds fly far from the house.

Lesson VIII.

THIRD CONJUGATION.

The base is formed by adding *ya* to the root. One of two changes takes place:

(*a*) *ya* may be added directly to the root, which ends in a vowel, *e.g.*, √gā to sing+ya=gāya; √jhā, to think+ya=jhāya

(*b*) *ya* may be assimilated to the final consonant of the root, according to the table of changes given below:—

Final	s+ya=ssa,	*e.g.*	√pas+ya=passa (to see)
,,	dh+ya=jjha	,,	√budh+ya=bujjha (to know)
,,	m+ya=mma	,,	√gam+ya=gamma (to go)
,,	c+ya=cca	,,	√ruc+ya=rucca (to be pleased)
,,	d+ya=jja	,,	√mad+ya=majja (to be intoxicated).
,,	ṇ+ya=ññа	,,	√bhaṇ+ya=bhañña (to say)
,,	n+ya=ñña	,,	√man+ya=mañña (to think)
,,	v+ya=bba	,,	√div+ya=dibba (to sport)
,,	h+ya=yha	,,	√sah+ya=sayha (to dare)

Feminine Nouns in i, ī.

Jāti—birth.

	Singular.	*Plural.*
Nom.	jāti.	jātī, jātiyo.
Gen. Dat.	jātiyā.	jātīnaṁ.
Acc.	jātiṁ.	jātī, jātiyo.

Ins. Abl.	jātiyā.	jātīhi.
Loc.	jātiyā, jātiyaṁ.	jātīsu.
Voc.	jāti,	jāti, jātiyo.

Note that jātiyā, jātiyaṁ may drop the *i*, thus giving jatyā jatyaṁ. (Generally a long vowel is not allowed before a double consonant. Hence the shortening of the vowel in jatyā, jatyam). According to a *sandhi* rule *ti*, *ty*, followed by a vowel becomes 'cc' Hence jatyā=jaccā; jatyaṁ=jaccaṁ. The student should note these changes.

Nadī—river.

	Singular.	*Plural.*
Nom.	nadī	nadī, nadiyo.
Gen. Dat.	nadiyā	nadīnaṁ.
Acc.	nadiṁ *nadiyam.*	nadī, nadiyo.
Ins. Abl	nadiyā.	nadīhi.
Loc.	nadiyā, nadiyaṁ.	nadīsu.
Voc.	nadi.	nadī, nadiyo.

Note *nadiyam* in the acc. sing.

On the analogy of jaccā, jaccaṁ, we have najjā, najjaṁ [d+y=jj, *see* Lesson VIII (*b*)]

FUTURE.

ss, the characteristic future sign is added between the root and the present suffixes, *e g.*

Singular	*Plural.*
1. pacissāmi.	pacissāma.
2. pacissasi.	pacissatha.
3. pacissati.	pacissanti.

Vocabulary of feminine nouns in *i*, *ī*;—ratti, night; bheri, drum; bhūmi, ground; iddhi, magical power; vuṭṭhi, rain; vīthi, road; siri, glory; satti, javelin; rati, pleasure; pīti, joy; itthī, woman; devī, queen; pokkharaṇī, tank; paccarī, raft; pathavī, earth; valli, creeper; bhisī, mat; bhaginī, sister.

Translations.—1. Sā mayhaṁ ruccati (this verb is construed with the gen.) 2. Seṭṭhino puttā vīthiyaṁ dibbissanti 3. Te migaṁ sihasmā muccissanti. 4. Tāyo amaccena saha gacchissanti. 5 Te vinā sakaṭena carissanti. 6. Amhākaṁ bhagini ratiṁ labhissati. 7. Mayaṁ suriyaṁ rattiyaṁ na passāma. 8. Te bheriṁ bhūmiyaṁ khipiṁsu.

1. The girl will see a gem on the arm of the sinner. 2. Run together with the elephant. 3. Sit on the raft with my son. 4. They will know (√budh) through magical powers. 5. Besmear the hand of the leper with medicine. 6. The lion will kill the deer. 7. They will see the glory of the queen. 8. The girl will throw the mat near the tank.

Lesson IX.

FOURTH CONJUGATION.

The base is obtained by adding to the root ṇo, ṇā or uṇo, uṇā, *e.g.*, √hi, to go—hiṇāti; √su, to listen—suṇoti, suṇāti; pāp (pa+√ap) to get, attain—pāpuṇāti; √vu, to restrain—vuṇāti.

MASCULINE *u* DECLENSION.

Ketu—banner.

	Singular	*Plural.*
Nom.	ketu.	ketū, ket*avo*.
Gen., Dat.	ketuno, ketussa.	ketūnaṁ.
Acc.	ketuṁ	ketū, ket*avo*.
Ins.	ketunā.	ketūhi.
Abl.	ketunā, ketusmā, ketumhā.	(ketūhi)
Loc.	ketumhi, ketusmiṁ.	ketūsu.
Voc.	ketu.	ketū, ketavo, ketave

Note the form *ketavo*.

Nouns. (like ketu) :—bhikkhu, monk; bindu, drop; hetu, cause; maccu, death; veḷu, bamboo; pharasu, hatchet; katacchu, spoon; setu, bridge.

PREFIXES.

A (before a consonant) } —*not*; as, agata, not gone;
An (before a vowel) } anācikkhita, not told.

Ati—*exceedingly*; as, atikaruṇā, excessive pity,

Adhi—*over, excessively, unto perfection*: as, adhikaroti does it perfectly.

Anu—*after, in imitation*; as, anudhāvati, runs after.

Anto—*within, interior*; as antonagaraṁ, in the town.

Apa—*off, away, in derision*; apagacchati, goes off; apavadati, insults.

Abhi—*to, excellently, towards*; as, abhigacchati, goes up to; abhimukho, facing; abhijānāti, knows well.

Ava (*or* o)— *way, down*; as, avagacchati, goes down.

Ā—*towards*; as, āpabbataṁ, towards the mountain. It very often reverses the meaning of some roots, as, ādāti, takes (√dā, to give); āgacchati, comes (√gam, to go).

Ud (*or* u)—*up*; as, uggacchati, goes up.

Upa—*below, towards*; as, uparājā, viceroy.

Du—*bad, difficult*; as, dudaso, difficult to see; dujjana, bad man.

Ni (before a consonant) } —*out, towards, down, without*; as, nisīdati, sits down; nigacchati, goes
Nir (before a vowel) } out; nirupakāra, useless.

Nī—*out*; as, nīharati, draws out.

Pa—*off, towards* (expressing *direction, origination*); as, pakkhandati, jumps forward.

Paṭi (*or* pati)—*against, opposite, in return*; as, paṭikaroti, repairs; paccāgacchati (pati+āgacchati), returns.

Parā—*opposite, in subjection*; as, parājayati, defeats.

Pāra—*beyond*; as pārasamudda, beyond the ocean.

Bahi—*outside*; as, bahigharaṁ, outside the house.

Vi—*away, different, excessively*; as, vigacchati, separates; viravati, shouts excessively.

Saṁ—*completely, well, with*; as, saṁharati, collects; sañjānāti, knows well.

Su—*good, well*; as, surūpa, good form; sujāta, well-born.

Translations:—1. Kaññā osadhaṁ pāpuṇissati 2. Te no apavadiṁsu. 3. Amaccā raṭṭhāni rakkhissanti 4. Bhikkhavo setumhi nipajjissanti. 5. Sīho migaṁ anudhāvati 6. Mayaṁ pārasamuddaṁ gacchissāma. 7. Tumhākaṁ puttā sakuṇehi saha kīḷanti (√kīḷ, *to play.*) 8. Mayaṁ tesaṁ uyyāne kīḷāma. 9. Kaññāya uyyāne udakaṁ piva (√pā, *to drink*).

1. They knew well the cause of the sound 2. Sit down near the minister's son. 3. They will kill the monk with an axe. 4. We shall eat together with the banker on the son's cart. 5. They ran after the elephant. 6. Eat your meal. 7. The viceroy killed the bad man (*dujjana, m.*) with a javelin. 8. They will return to thet own with the ministers 9. Lie down in the garden of the minister.

Lesson X.

FIFTH CONJUGATION.

The base is obtained by adding *nā* to the root; as, √ci, to heap—cinā; √ji, to conquer—jinā; √as, to eat—asnā; √yu, to mix—yunā; √jā, to know—Jānā.

OPTATIVE.

	Singular.	*Plural.*
1.	paceyyāmi.	paceyyāma.
2.	paceyyāsi.	paceyyātha.
3.	paceyya, pace. ✝	paceyyuṁ.

Feminine U Declension.

Dhenu—"cow."

	Singular.	*Plural.*
Nom.	dhenu	dhenū ; dhenuyo.
Gen. Dat.	dhenuyā	dhenūnaṁ.
Acc.	dhenuṁ	dhenū ; dhenuyo.
Ins. Abl.	dhenuyā	dhenūhi
Loc.	dhenuyā ; dhenuyaṁ	dhenūsu.
Voc.	dhenu	dhenū ; dhenuyo.

Nouns (like dhenu).

Dhātu—"sacred relic."	Sassu—"mother-in-law."
Rajju—"string," "rope."	Yāgu—"rice gruel."

Usu—"arrow."

Neuter I and U Declension.

(*a*) Aṭṭhi—"bone."

	Singular.	*Plural.*
Nom.	aṭṭhi ; aṭṭhiṁ	aṭṭhīni.
Gen. Dat.	aṭṭhino; aṭṭhissa	aṭṭhīnaṁ.
Acc.	aṭṭhiṁ	aṭṭhīni.
Ins.	aṭṭhinā	aṭṭhihi.
Abl.	aṭṭhinā ; aṭṭhimhā ; aṭṭhismā	aṭṭhihi.
Loc.	aṭṭhimhi ; aṭṭhismiṁ	aṭṭhisu.
Voc.	aṭṭhi	aṭṭhīni.

Vocabulary.

Akkhi—"eye."	Satthi—"thigh."
Sappi—"butter ;" "ghee."	Vāri—"water."

(*b*) Cakkhu—"eye."

	Singular.	*Plural.*
Nom.	cakkhu ; cakkhuṁ	cakhkūni.

	Singular	Plural
Gen. Dat.	cakkhuno ; cukkhussa	cakkhūnaṁ.
Acc.	cakkhuṁ	cakkhūni.
Ins.	cakkhunā	cakkhūhi.
Abl.	cakkhunā ; cakkhumhā, cakkhusmā.	
Loc.	cakkhumhi ; cakkhumiṁ	cakkhūsu.
Voc.	cakkhu	cakkhūni.

VOCABULARY.

Assu—" tear."
Ayu—" life."
Dāru—" fire-wood ; " " fire stick."

Note :—There are no neuter nouns in ī, ū.

Mas. and fem. nouns in ū, are like the corresponding forms in u and need not be treated separately, *e.g.* vadhū, *f* a widow—gen. vadhuyā, etc.

CONNECTIVES AND CORRELATIVES.

Ca—*and*
vā—*or* } used between words and phrases.

Sace, ce—*if* :—used in complex sentences.

Pana—*but*
udāhu—*or* } used in compound sentences.

hi—*because, indeed,* generally follows the main word in the sentence.

Ca...........ca, *both...........and*
na...........na, *neither...........nor.*
vā...........vā, *either...........or.*
yadā, *when*—tadā, *then.*
yathā, *as*—tathā, *so.*
yattha, *where*—tattha, *there.*
pana.—*as for, but for.*
yāva, yāvatā—*as far, until.*
tāva, tāvatā—*so far, till then.*

Note :—Ca, ce and pana are never used at the beginning of a sentence.

Ce and pana are generally placed immediately after the first word or the subject in the sentence.

Sace may be used to begin a sentence.

Examples:—Amacco ca putto ca—both minister and son. One *ca* may be omitted, as, amacco ca putto or amacco putto ca. *Ca* may be omitted altogether.

Amacco vā putto vā
amacco vā putto
amacco putto vā } —either minister or son

Sace so āgacchati ahaṁ nisīdissāmi
So sace (*or* ce) āgacchati ahaṁ nisīdissāmi } if he comes I will sit down.

Pāpakārī hi socati—indeed an evil-doer grieves.

Ahaṁ paceyyāmi so pana maṁ rundhi, I would cook but he prevented me.

Yadā so āgacchati tadā bhuñjissāmi—when he comes I will eat.

Yathā so nâgacchati (na + āgacchati) tathā karissāmi—I will act so that he may not come.

Yattha tumhe kaññaṁ passatha, tattha nisīdatha, where you see the girl, there sit down.

Yāva so Buddhaṁ passi tāva nipajji, as long as he could see the Buhdha, so long he lay down.

Translations:—1. When you see him, ask for his cart. 2. So long as the girl does not sit down, so long she will not see the queen. 3 My sister and her son went together with his queen. 4 They would not sit on the mat. 5. Throw the gem into the garden. 6, If he comes, we may go to the river. 7. When you see them in the garden, tell me so. 8 Eat so long as you can get food. 9. They would kill the elephant with the javelin, but I prevented them. 10. Go to the queen's garden with my son and sister.

Lesson XI.

SIXTH CONJUGATION.

The base is obtained by adding *o* to the root. The student should remember that *o* is the *guna* or strong form of u, ū and *e* of i, ī. The semi-vowel of u, u is *av* and of i, ī is *ay*, *e.g.* √kar. to do—karo ; √tan. to stretch – tano; √van, to beg—vano.

IMPERFECT.

	Singular.	*Plural.*
1.	apaca, apacaṁ.	apacamhā.
2.	apaco.	apacattha.
3.	apaca	apacu.

Note the augment *a*, which is also used in the aorist and the conditional (see further).

INTERJECTIONS.

Alaṁ, enough ! Je, sir !
Vata, surely ! indeed! Sādhu, well done !
Handa, come ! pray ! Bhaṇe, I say !
Maññe, I suppose ! Ambho, look here !
Re are, man ! you fellow !

Note : – alaṁ is construed with the instrumentive *e.g.*, alaṁ ambehi —enough of mangoes.

VOCATIVES.

Amma—mother, madam.

Ayya—sir.

Ayyā, ayye,—madam.

Avuso – sir (used by monks of equal seniority to each other or by senior monks to junior monks.)

Ayasmā - - sir (used by junior monks to senior monks).

Bhadda, bhadde—my dear girl, good wife.

Bho—sir, madam.

Bhante (same as āyasmā in use.)

Deva—Lord, Your Majesty, Sire.

Devī—Lady, Your Majesty.

Tāta—beloved, dear, darling.

Samma—friend, dear fellow.

Translations:—1. Amacco veriṁ jineyya. 2. Raṭṭhaṁ vo gaccheyya. 3. Sace te sīhaṁ passeyyuṁ taṁ anudhāveyyuṁ. 4. Buddhassa santike osadhaṁ labheyyuṁ. 5. Passa, dhāvati. 6. So mama raṭṭhaṁ agā 7. Kaññāyo nāvāya āgu. 8. Putto cetiyaṁ agamā. 9. Te sakaṭena agamū. 10. So bhikkhuno osadhaṁ adā.

1. The son went to the king by boat. 2. They saw a lion in the garden. 3. Sit down sir! 4. Friend, go with my son 5. My dear, let the minister protect your son. 6. Either he or his son will come to your house. 7 Neither my sister nor the queen sat down near him. 8. Both the evil-doer and the bad man will go to hell (*niraya, m.*) 9. Enough of your talk (*Sallāpa, m.*) 10. I say, you must come to my house to-morrow (*sve, adv.*)

Lesson XII.

SEVENTH CONJUGATION.

The base is formed by adding *e* or *aya* to the root. Generally the vowel of the root is strengthened, *e.g.*, √kath, to speak—kathe, kathaya; √cur, to steal—core, coraya; √gup, to guard—gope, gopaya; √tir, to cross—tīre, tīraya; √pus, to nourish—pose, posaya; √chaḍḍ, to reject—chaḍḍe, chaḍḍaya.

CONDITIONAL.

	Singular.	*Plural.*
1.	apacissaṁ	apacissamhā.
2.	apacisse, apacissa.	apacissatha.
3.	apacissā, apacissa.	apacissaṁsu.

ADJECTIVES.

These agree with the nouns they qualify in gender, number and case, as, bālo putto, a foolish son; bālena puttena, by a foolish son; bālā kaññā, a foolish girl; bālāya kaññāya, by a foolish girl; sundaraṁ raṭṭhaṁ, a beautiful country; sundarena raṭṭhena, through a beautiful country.

It will thus be seen that most adjectives are declined like *putta* in the masculine, *kaññā* in the feminine and *gharaṁ* in the neuter.

Vocabulary:—Sacca, true; mahallaka, old; pāpa, evil; kusala, meritorious; sītala, cool; dīgha, long; paṇḍita, clever; sukha, happy; dukkha, painful.

Adjectives may be compounded with nouns. Thus, paṇḍitapuriso a, wise man; pāpakammaṁ, a sinful deed; pharusavacanaṁ, a harsh speech.

Adjectives ending in i, ī, u, ū (like bhuri, abundant; mānī, proud; bahu, many; kataññū, grateful) are declined like the corresponding nouns in i, ī, u ū.

Translations:—1. Sace so raṭṭhaṁ alabhissā kusalaṁ bhāveyya. 2. Sace so pabbajjaṁ (*f. ordination*) alabhissā arahā (*Saint*) abhavissā. 3. Sace mayaṁ veriṁ apassissaṁsu taṁ avadhissaṁsu. 4. Sace sā rathaṁ (*m, chariot*) alabhissā amaccassa raṭṭhaṁ agacchissā. 5. Ahaṁ mahallakassa purisassa gharasmiṁ nipajjiṁ. 6. Te pāpakammāni karonti. Bālo puriso nirayaṁ gacchissati. 8. Te kusalāni kammāni karonti. 9. Kaññāyo sītalāyaṁ chāyāyaṁ nisīdiṁsu. 10. Te dīghaṁ addhānaṁ (*n, time*) nipajjiṁsu.

1. Kill the foolish minister. 2. If we could get a cart, we could go with them 3. They saw an old man on the bridge. 4. Do meritorious deeds. 5. One should not do bad deed, (*use the optative*) 6 Either you or she must see me. 7. If you would cook the rice, I would eat it. 8.

They played with the foolish girls. 9. I stole a mango from his garden. 10. We shall cross the ocean tomorrow.

Lesson XIII.

PARTICIPLES.

Participles are like adjectives and agree with the nouns they qualify in gender, number and case.

Present participle active is obtained by adding *nta* to the base, *e.g.*, pacanta (mas.), pacantı (fem.), pacantaṁ (neu.) The masculine and neuter also have a common form pacaṁ. The masculine is declined like *putta*, the feminine like *nadi* and the neuter. like *gharaṁ*.

The stem of the present participle is in *at* or *ant*. Hence we have pacant-a, pacant-i, pacant-aṁ from the stem in *ant*. From the stem in *at* we have in the feminine pacat-i, which is declined in full like pacantī, the only difference being the absence of *n* before *t*. And in the masculine. and neuter we have some special forms which ought to be noted carefully.

	Singular.	*Plural.*
Nom.	pacaṁ	
Gen. Dat.	pacat-*o*	pacat-aṁ.
Ins. Abl.	pacat-ā	
Loc.	pacat-i	

Hence the full declension of the present participle is as follows :—

Singular.

	Mas.	Fem.	Neu.
Nom.	pacaṁ	pacatī	pacaṁ.
	pacanto	pacantī	pacantaṁ.

Gen. Dat.	pacato pacantassa	pacatiyā pacantiyā	pacato. pacantassa.
Acc.	pacantaṁ	pacatiṁ pacantiṁ	pacantaṁ.
Ins.	pacatā pacantena	pacatiyā pacantiyā	pacatā. pacantena.
Abl	pacatā pacantasmā pacantamhā	pacatiyā pacantiyā	pacatā. pacantasmā. pacantamhā.
Loc.	pacati pacante pacantasmiṁ pacantamhi	pacatiyā pacantiyā pacatiyaṁ pacantiyaṁ	pacati. pacante. pacantasmim. pacantamhi.
Voc.	pacaṁ pacanta	pacatī pacantī	pacam. pacanta.

Plural.

Nom.	pacantā	pacatī pacatiyo pacantī pacantiyo	pacantāni.
Gen. Dat.	pacatam pacantānaṁ	pacatīnaṁ pacantīnaṁ	pacataṁ. pacantānaṁ.
Acc.	pacante pacantā	pacatiyo pacatī pacanti pacantiyo	pacantāni.
Ins. Abl.	pacantehi pacantebhi	pacatīhi pacatībhi pacantīhi pacantībhi	pacantehi. pacantebhi.
Loc.	pacantesu	pacatīsu pacantīsu	pacantesu.

Voc.	pacantā	pacatī pacatiyo pacantī pacantiyo	pacantāni.

Rājā—king, is declined somewhat on the lines of these special forms, so also are pitā—father, and similar words mostly denoting relationship, *viz.*, mātā—mother, bhātā,—brother, bhattā—husband, nattā—grandson, satthā—teacher.

Rājā—king.

	Singular.	*Plural.*
Nom.	rājā	rājā, rājāno.
Gen. Dat.	rañño	raññaṁ, rājūnaṁ.
Acc.	rājānaṁ	rājā, rājāno.
Ins. Abl.	raññā	rājūhi.
Loc.	raññe (a+i)	rājūsu.
Voc.	rāja	rājā, rājāno.

Note:—Compounds of rājā like mahārājā—emperor, devarājā—king of gods, uparājā—viceroy, etc., may also be declined in the ordinary way like *putta*, except the nom. *e.g.*, nom. sing.—mahārājā; gen.—mahārājassa, mahārañño; gen. pl.—mahārājānaṁ, mahāraññaṁ.

Pitā—father.

	Singular.	*Plural.*
Nom.	pitā	pitaro.
Gen. Dat.	pitussa, pituno	pitunnaṁ, pitūnaṁ, pitarānaṁ.
Acc.	pitaraṁ	pitaro.
Ins. Abl.	pitarā	pitūhi, pitarehi.
Loc.	pitari	pitūsu, pitaresu.
Voc.	pita	pitaro.

Mātā—mother. (fem.)

	Singular.	*Plural.*
Nom.	mātā	mātaro.
Gen. Dat.	mātu, mātuyā	mātarānaṁ, mātūnaṁ, mātunnaṁ.
Acc.	mātaraṁ	mātaro
Ins. Abl.	mātarā	mātarehi, mātūhi.
Loc.	mātari	mātaresu, mātūsu.
Voc.	māta	mātaro.

Bhātā, brother; bhattā, husband; nattā, grandson; satthā, teacher, are declined like pitā except that the vowel *a* before *ram, ru, ro* is long being after a double consonant, as, bhattāraṁ, bhattāro, bhattārā. Dhitā, daughter is declined like mātā. Note that the base of these words ends in *u*, as pitu, mātu, etc. and the nom. in *ā*.

Mātāpitaro—father and mother, parents.

(base—mātāpitu).

Nom.	mātāpitaro.
Gen. Dat.	mātāpitūnaṁ, mātāpitunnaṁ.
Acc.	mātāpitaro.
Ins. Abl.	mātāpitūhi.
Loc.	mātāpitūsu.
Voc.	mātāpitaro.

Translations:—1. Ahaṁ satthāraṁ raṭṭhaṁ gacchantaṁ passiṁ 2. Sā bhattaṁ pacanti mari. 3. Mahārājassa putto vithiyaṁ (vīthi *road f.*) gacchanto kaññaṁ vadhi. 4. So tehi saddhiṁ kīḷanto puttaṁ anudhāvi. 5. So mama raṭṭhe, carantassa purisassa santike nipajji. 6. Mātāpitūnam ovādaṁ (*m*, advice) suṇeyya. 7. Pitarā saha gacchantaṁ puttaṁ pakkosi (√ kus—call.) 8. Mama bhātā ca bhattā tesaṁ nagaraṁ sve āgacchissanti. 9. Mayaṁ satthāraṁ vandissāma (√vand—to salute). 10. Tàssa kathaṁ suṇātha.

1. We saw a man running after the deer in the king's garden. 2. Going along the road they spoke to a man sitting down near a shrine. 3. Sit in the king's presence. 4. He did meritorious deeds. 5. The king's daughters and sons came to my country. 6. They ran after a lion killing an elephant. 7. The woman playing with her grandson died in my house. 8. You should listen to the king's advice. 9. Going along the road they killed a lion. 10. Certainly he saw him lying down in the shade of the tree (*rukkha*, m.)

Lesson XIV.

PERFECT.

The root is reduplicated according to the rules (*see* Lesson VI).

Singular.	*Plural.*
1. papaca	papacimha.
2. papace	papacittha.
3. papaca	papacu.

Present Participle Reflexive.

The sign *māna* is added to the base, *e g.*, pacamāna. It is declined like putta (*m.*) kaññā (*f.*) and gharaṁ (*neu.*)

It has much the same meaning as the participle active. A variant form of it is obtained by adding *āna* to the root, *e.g.*, pacāno, pacānā, pacānaṁ.

The use of so, sa, taṁ as adjectives.

So, sā, taṁ and their cases become demonstrative adjectives when they are placed before nouns.

Mas. { so puriso—that man.
tehi purisehi—by these men, etc.

Fem. { sā kaññā—that girl.
tāyaṁ kaññāyaṁ—in that girl.

Neu. { taṁ gharaṁ—that house.
tesu gharesu—in those houses.

If *e* is put before them, they mean *this*, *e.g.*

eso puriso—this man.
esā kaññā—this girl.
etaṁ gharaṁ—this house.

Translations:—1. So amacco odanaṁ (*rice*) papaca 2. Bhikkhūnaṁ dānaṁ dadattha. 3. Ahaṁ taṁ. purisaṁ nagarasmā āgacchamānaṁ passiṁ. 4. Esā kāññā odanaṁ pacānā mari. 5. Te bhikkhavo satthārā saddhim etasmiṁ gharamhi nipajjiṁsu. 6. Esā dhītā mātarā saha kiḷamānā pati. 7. Esā nadi sundarā. 8. Eso puriso rañño mahantaṁ rathaṁ coreti. 9. Te mahisā (*m, buffalo*) tesu āvāṭesu (*m, pit*) patiṁsu. 10. Mahārājā purohite (*m, chaplain*) tesaṁ amaccānaṁ pahiṇati (√hi, *sends*).

1. Kill that man running after that girl. 2. Sit down on that raft. 3. If I see you playing with that minister's son, I will kill you. 4. If you do bad deeds, I shall not come to your house. 5. They are not coming with my son. 6. Send those boys (*dāraka, m*) to the king's palace (*pāsāda, m*). 7. The chaplain desires money (*rūpiya, n.*) 8. Those women lay down in that pit. 9. My son and his daughter stayed in that house. 10. They slept (*niddāyati*) on that bridge.

Lesson XV.

PERFECT PARTICIPLE PASSIVE.

This is formed by adding *ta* or *na* to the root; *ta* may be added in three ways:—

(*a*) joined directly to the root, which ends in a vowel, *e.g.*, √bhū—bhūta, √nī—nīta, √ji—jita.

(*b*) joined by means of the connecting vowel *i* to the root, which ends in a consonant, as √pac—pacita, √kath—kathita, √likh—likhita.

(*c*) the *t* of *ta* being assimilated to the last consonant of the root, when certain changes take place, as follows :—

final j+ta=tta, as, √bhuj+ta=bhutta.
final c+ta=tta, as, √muc+ta=mutta.
final p+ta=tta, as, √tap+ta=tatta.
final t+ta=tta, as, √pat+ta=patta.
final s+ta=ṭṭha, as, √kas+ta=kaṭṭha.
final m+ta=nta, as, √gam+ta=ganta.
final dh+ta=ddha, as, √budh+ta=buddha.
final bh+ta=ddha, as, √labh+ta=laddha.
final h+ta=ḷha, as, √ruh+ta=ruḷha.

Note:—Final *n* and *r* are generally dropped before *ta* *e.g.*, √khan—khata; √kar—kata.

Sometimes final *m* is also dropped, as, √gam—gata. These participles in the neuter from are often used as nouns, *e.g.*, √jīv—to live, jīvitaṁ—life; √has—to smile, hasitaṁ—a smile.

Note also that the *p.p.p.* is very often used as a finite verb, as, So nagaraṁ gato, he has gone or went to town.

na is less common and generally added to roots in *d*, *r*, when assimilation takes place, *e.g.* √chid—chinna, √chad—channa, ni √sad—nisinna; √tar—tiṇṇa, √kir—kiṇṇa.

Note the change of the radical vowel and also that 'n' is dotted or becomes a cerebral owing to the influence of the preceding 'r.' Other examples of the influence of 'r' will be met with rather frequently and the student should recognize it. Also √bhaj+na=bhagga, √lag+na=lagga, √vij+na=vigga.

Sometimes *na* may be added directly, *e.g.*, √lū—lūna, √lī—līna, √hā—hīna.

N. B.—An active sentence is often turned into passive by using the *p.p.p. e.g. I have done merit* is turned into *merit has been done by me*=kusalaṁ mayā kataṁ. This is an important use of the *p.p.p.* and should be carefully noted.

Translations:—1. Dhammo bhikkhūhi suto. 2. Raṭṭhaṁ puttena jitaṁ 3. Sā kaññā sakaṭena tesaṁ gharaṁ gatā. 4. Amhehi kusalaṁ akataṁ. 5. Gharaṁ agginā ādiṭṭhaṁ. 6. Sā bhaṇḍika (*bundle*) tasmā pabbatasmā patitā. 7. Te 7 manussa etesaṁ āsanānaṁ (*n, seat*) heṭṭho niddāyiṁsu. 8. Tasmiṁ raṭṭhe so uparājā sangāme (*m, battle*) parājito (*defeated*). 9. Amhākaṁ pituno etāni sākaṭāni dadāhi. 10. Ete koṭṭhāsā (*divsion*, tāyaṁ bhaṇḍikāyaṁ taṁ purisaṁ mayā dinnā.

1. We have not done good deeds. 2. They went to town on the king's elephant. 3. We saw a man seated on a raft. 4. They have eaten our food. 5. A bird has been killed by the hunter. 6. Evil doers will go to hell. 7. They saw a man dead in the house. 8. The king has been defeated by the enemy (veri, *m.*) 9. Those girls sat in these seats. 10. A heap of jewels has been stolen by these men.

Lesson XVI.

RELATIVE AND INTERROGATIVE PRONOUNS.

Yo (relative)—who, which, what.

MASCULINE.

	Singular.	*Plural.*
Nom.	yo	ye.
Gen. Dat.	yassa	yesaṁ.
Acc.	yaṁ	ye.
Ins.	yena	yehi.
Abl.	yasmā, yamhā	(yehi.)
Loc.	yasmiṁ, yamhi	yesu.

FEMININE.

Nom.	yā	yā, yāyo.
Gen. Dat.	yāya, yassā	yāsaṁ.
Acc.	yaṁ	yā, yāyo.
Ins. Abl.	yāya	yāhi.
Loc.	yāyaṁ, yassaṁ	yāsu.

NEUTER.

Nom.	yaṁ	yāni.
Gen. Dat.	yassa	yesaṁ.
Acc.	yaṁ	yāni.
Ins.	yena	} vehi.
Abl.	yasmā, yamhā	
Loc.	yasmiṁ, yamhi	yesu.

Indefinite pronouns declined like *ya* :—

añña itara para	} other, another	aññatara, a certain, some pubba, former sabba, all.

Note that the nom. pl. of these pronouns ends in *e*.

Ka (Interrogative)—who, which, what?

Decline *ka* in exactly the same way as *ya*, except that the neuter nom. sing. and acc. is *kiṁ* not *kaṁ*, *eg.*, kiṁ karissati? What will he do?

Note that the *ṁ* of kiṁ being niggahita is changed to nasal according to the rule of sandhi (Lesson VII) o· *m* before a vowel, as, so kim akāsi? What did he Kin te kataṁ? What has been done by thee?

Kiṁ with the dative and instrumentive.

When *kim* is used with the dative of a person and the instrumentive of a thing, action, state or other circumstances, it means " where is the use of?" as,

Kin te puttena? Where is the use of a so· thee?

Kim me āgacchantena—there is no use in ... coming?

This use of *kiṁ* should be noted. When in such a sentence *kim* is replaced by *attho*, the sentence means—*There is need of something to somebody, e.g*

Attho me kapinā—I have need of a monkey.

Attho te rajjena—Thou hast need of sovereignty.

In the negative *n'atthi* (*there is not*) is used, as,

Attho me kapinā n'atthi—I have no need of a monkey.

Kiṁ may be compounded with a following noun, as,

Kimpasaddhā—what faith?
Kiṅkāranā (*abl*)—what cause? Why?

Ya as correlative.

(*a*) Ya is used with so, sā, taṁ as a correlative, as,—
Yo puriso tena saddhiṁ gacchi so mari—the man with whom he went died.

Yasmiṁ gharasmiṁ so nipajjissati tasmiṁ gh miṁ ahaṁ vasissāmi—In the house where he will lie down, I shall live.

Yā itthī taṁ purisaṁ pakkosati sā ativiya bālā—the woman who calls that man is very foolish

(*b*) acc. *yaṁ*, ins. *yena*, abl, *yasmā* are used adverb ially meaning *since*, *because*, as,—

Tumhe taṁ na vadheyyātha yaṁ so paṇḍito—You might not kill him because he was clever.

Yasmā so maṁ pahari tasmā na tena saha gacchāmi—because he struck me therefore I do not go with him.

Taṁ karanaṁ suṇohi yena kāraṇena so mari—Listen to the reason why he died.

Yena...tena is used with a verb of motion to denote destination, as,

Yena Bhagavā ten' upasaṅkami—He approached the Buddha.

INDEFINITE PRONOUNS.

By adding *ci* (*cid*), *api*, *cana*, *canaṁ* to *ko*, *kā*, *kim* and their casé-forms, we get indefinite pronouns, meaning whoever, whatever, anyone.

Ci is the one mostly used, *e.g.*, koci puriso—whatever man.

Koci (mas.)—whatever, anyone.

	Singular.	*Plural.*
Nom.	koci.	keci.
Gen. Dat.	kassaci.	kesañci.
Acc.	kañci, kiñci.	keci.
Ins.	kenaci	kehici.
Abl.	kasmāci	
Loc.	kasmiñci, kamhici kismiñci, kimhici	kesuci.

Kāci (fem).

Nom.	kāci.	kāci, kāyoci.
Gen. Dat.	kāyaci, kassāci.	kāsañci.
Acc.	kañci.	kāci, kāyoci.
Ins. Abl.	kāyaci.	kāhici.
Loc.	kāyaci, kāyañci kassañci.	kāsuci.

The neuter is like the masc. except in the nom. acc. sing. we have kiñci and in the plural kānici.

Translations:—1. The girl is in need of medicine. 2. Where is the use of your coming with my son? 3. The lion went to where the deer was sleeping. 4. Why do you commit bad deeds? 5. We have done a very bad deed. 6. Whoever comes to my house is a thief. 7. The girl whom you see with him is my sister. 8. The men who called me are his brothers. 9. Do you know the reason why he is mad (*ummattaka*)? 10. In whatever place (*padesa*, *m.*) you see him, strike him on the head (*matthaka*, m.).

Lesson XVII.

GERUND.

Compound sentences joined by "and" are denoted by the gerund. *e g.*

Kaññā taṇḍulaṁ p citvā bhuñjitvā nipajji—the girl cooked rice, ate and lay down. *or* The girl having cooked rice and eaten lay down.

One of the suffixes, is *tvā*, which like the *ta* of the *p.p.p.*, may be added in three ways:

(*a*) directy added to the root in a vowel, as, √su—sutvā.

(*b*) by means of connecting vowel 'i', as, √pac—pacitvā

(*c*) by assimilation, as, √gam—gantvā; √bhuj—bhutvā, √kar—katvā (*r* being dropped.)

Sometimes the radical vowel is strengthened, as √nī—netvā.

Tvāna and *tūna* are less common, being mostly used in poetry.

Ya is another gerundial suffix, chiefly used when the root takes a prefix, as, ā√dā—ādāya (directly); ā√gam—āgamma (assimilation).

It may be joined by means of 'i', as, √pac—paciya.

It may also be added to the base, as, √bhuj—bhuñjiya.

N.B.—The tense of the gerund depends on the tense of the finite verb, as—

(*a*) So taṇḍulaṁ pacitvā khāditvā gacchati—He goes having cooked rice and eaten it (*present.*)

(*b*) So taṇḍulaṁ pacitvā khāditvā gacchissati (*future.*)

(*c*) So taṇḍulaṁ pacitvā khāditvā gacchi (*aorist*).

(*d*) So taṇḍulaṁ pacitvā khāditvā gaccheyya (*optative.*)

(*e*) Taṇḍulaṁ pacitvā khāditvā gaccha (*imperative*) Having cooked rice and eaten it, go.

These examples will help the student in the right use of the gerund in translating into Pali. Thus all those actions denoted by verbs in English are to be put into gerunds except the last, which must be a finite verb, having the tense given in English. The sentence (*e*) above would also mean—Cook rice, eat and go; which, however, is exactly the same in sense as—Having cooked rice and eaten it go. The student should not be puzzled by different expressions in English, if he observed the Pali form. But such a sentence as *Come and see me* being infinitive of purpose in sense would be better translated by the infinite; thus— *Come to see me*— maṁ passituṁ āgaccha.

There is another form of ya and that is *tya* which with a preceding vowel regularly becomes *cca*. (see p. 14 *e.g.* pa √i, to go + tya = petya = pecca.

INFINITIVE.

Tum is the sign, which is added in three ways. It should be remarked that suffixes beginning with *t*, as the *p.p.p.* gerund and infinitive, are on the whole treated in the same way. Hence the three ways of joining the *p.p.p.* to the root serve also for the gerund and the infinitive. Of course there are little variations. But the broad general principle should not be missed. Hence also the table of assimilation of *ta* (Lesson XV) applies, making allowances for special changes in each, also for the gerund, infinitive and practically for all suffixes which begin with *t*.

(*a*) directly, as √dā—dātuṁ.
(*b*) by 'i', a, √pac—pacituṁ.
(*c*) by assimilation, as, √labh—laddhuṁ.

The last consonant may be dropped, as √kar—kātuṁ.

This is an instance of the law of compensation, owing to which the vowel *a* is lengthened to compensate for the loss of *r*.

i, ī. u, ū, are lengthened into *e*, *o*, as,—

√ji—jetuṁ or jayituṁ.

√su—sotuṁ or savituṁ.

In poetry *tave* may be used, as, √ha, hātave; the infinitive expresses *purpose*.

Translations:—1. Ahaṁ odanaṁ pacitvā khādituṁ ārabhāmi. 2. Vāṇijo dhanaṁ laddhuṁ vicarati. 3. So paccariyaṁ nipajjitvā mari. 4. Mama putto bhikkhuṁ passitvā dhammaṁ suṇāti. 5. Kaññā ācariyaṁ (*m*, *teacher*) pucchitvā āgacchati. 6. Luddo migaṁ vadhituṁ aṭaviṁ pavisati (√vis *enters*). 7 Mahārājā veriṁ jetuṁ saṅgāme yujjhati (√yudh, *to fight*) 8. Te purisā bhattaṁ khādituṁ nisīdiṁsu. 9. Te mama puttassa jīvitaṁ rakkheyyuṁ. 10. Satthāraṁ pañhaṁ pucchituṁ gaccha.

1. The merchants go about to get a cart. 2. Sit down to see the minister eating rice. 3. Having sat down he cooked the food for somebody. 4. He came to town to see the king and queen. 5. Having seen them seated on the ground they went away. 6. They were playing when I saw them. 7. The king's elephant has arrived. 8. Come and see my pretty bird. 9. Those girls and these boys will play together in my garden. 10. I have no need of your food.

Lesson XVIII.

PASSIVE.

This is formed by adding *ya* to the root in three ways:—

(*a*) directly, as, √nī—nīya, √ bhū—bhūya.

Roots in ā change the vowel into ī, as, √dā—dīya, √pā—pīya—

(*b*) by means of *i*, the root ending in a consonant, and *i* being lengthened into *ī*., as √sar—sarīya, √has—hasīya (*c*) by assimilation (see assimilation of *ya*, Lesson VIII.) √labh—labbha, √han—haññа.

Some passive verbs are formed on the special base, as, √is—icch (base)—icchiya ; √gam—gacch (base)—gacchiya.

To the base thus formed are added the personal endings of the tense wanted, *e.g.*

√ji—jiya (pass. base)—jiyeyyāmi—I should be conquered.

NUMERALS.

Eka—'one' is declined like *so* in the masculine and like *gharaṁ* in the neuter, and almost like *sa* in the feminine.

Ekā (fem.) One.

	Singular.	*Plural.*
Nom.	ekā	ekā, ekāyo
Gen. Da.	ekissā. ekāya	ekānaṁ
Acc.	ekaṁ	ekā, ekāyo
Ins. Abl.	ekissā, ekāya	ekāhi
Loc.	ekissā, ekissāyaṁ ekāya, ekāyaṁ	ekāsn

Note the that plural forms mean *some*, *e.g.*

Eke purisā— some men.

Other numerals are declined as follows :—

Base.	Nom. & Acc.	Gen. & Dat.	Ins. & Abl.	Loc.
dvi, di (*two*)	dve	dvinnaṁ	dvīhi	dvisu.
ti (*three*) ...	*mas.* tayo *fem.* tisso *neu.* tini	tiṇṇaṁ tissannaṁ tiṇṇaṁ	tīhi	tisu.
catu (*four*)	*mas.* cattāro *fem.* catasso *neu.* cattāri	catuṇṇaṁ catassannaṁ catuṇṇaṁ	catūhi	catūsu.
pañca (*five*)	pañca	pañcannaṁ	pancahi	pancasu.

Cha, six ; satta, seven ; aṭṭha, eight ; nava, nine ; dasa, ten ; ekādasa, eleven ; dvādasa, twelve ; terasa, thirteen ; catuddasa, fourteen ; pañcadasa, fifteen ; soḷasa, sixteen ; sattadasa, seventeen ; aṭṭhadasa, eighteen—are declined like *panca*.

Ekūnavīsati, 19 (eka+ūna+vīsati) ; vīsati, 20 up to 99 are declined like the feminines in *i*, like *jāti*.

e.g. Asitiyaṁ purisesu—among eighty men

Sata, hundred ; sahassaṁ, thousand are declined like *gharam*. They generally govern the genitive, as, purisānaṁ sahassaṁ—a thouand men.

Ordinals.

mas.	*fem.*	*new.*
(declined like *Putta*)	(like fem. in ā, ī)	(like *gharam*)
Paṭhamo (*first*)	paṭhamā	paṭhamam
Dutiyo (*second*)	dutiyā	dutiyaṁ.
Tatiyo (*third*)	tatiyā	tatiyaṁ.
Catuttho (*fourth*)	catutthī	catutthaṁ

Pañcamo (*fifth*)	pañcamī	pañcamaṁ.
Chaṭṭho } (*sixth*)	caṭṭhī }	caṭṭhaṁ.
Chaṭṭhamo }	catthami }	chaṭṭhaṁ.
Sattamo (*seventh*)	sattam	sattamaṁ.
Aṭṭhamo (*eighth*)	aṭṭhamī	aṭṭhamaṁ.
Navamo (*ninth*)	navamī	navamaṁ.
Dasamo (*tenth*)	dasamī	dasamaṁ.
etc.	etc.	etc.

Translations:—1. Te tayo puttā nagarasmā gacchanti 2. Eso rājā tīṇi sakaṭāni vikkiṇatī (*to sell*). 3. Dve purisā ca catasso itthiyo ekasmiṁ ghare nipajjanti. 4. Tena amaccena kusalaṁ kammaṁ karīyati. 5. Cattāro purisā ca catasso kaññāyo ekissā rattiyaṁ gacchanti. 6. Sabbe manussā sotthiṁ (f *prosperity*) labhantu. 7 Aññataro devo (*m. god*) tassā kaññāya maṅgalaṁ (*n blessing*) dadāti. 8 Itaro aṭaviyaṁ antaradhāyati (√dhā, to disappear). Etā. tisso itthiyo mahantaṁ yasaṁ (*m. fame*) pāpuṇanti. 10. Eso senāpati (*m general*) mahantiyā senāya cattāri raṭṭhāni parājito.

1. I saw four men killing two deer. 2. Run after those two men. 3. On a raft sat five men. 4. Five girls are killed by two men. 5. The deer is brought by two men. 6. All must alute the general. 7. The first man whom you see there came to me at night. 8. The second cart has been sold by my wife. 9. I was struck on my arm by two girls. 10. Sit down in the tenth seat.

Lesson XIX

CAUSATIVE VERBS.

These are formed by *e, aya, āpe* or *āpaya* joined to the root. The vowel preceding these suffixes is lengthened, *e.g.*, √pac—pāceti, pācayati, pacāpeti or pacāpayati. The true suffixes really are *e* or āpe. But since e = aya we get also āpe = āpaya.

Roots which form bases in *e* take āpe to become causative, as kathe (√kath)—kathāpeti, kathāpayati.

Roots in i, ī, u, ū form the causative from the base, as √su—sāveti, √sī—sāyeti.

Causative Verbs may govern two accusatives, as, Ahaṁ kaññaṁ bhattaṁ pācessāmi—I shall cause the girl to cook the food.

Roots in ā also take āpe as, √dā—dāpeti. But √ṭhā—ṭhapeti.

COMPARISON OF ADJECTIVES.

This is formed by adding to the positive *tara* for the comparative and *tama* for the superlative; as, pāpa—pāpatara—pāpatama.

Comparison is also expressed by adding to the positive *iya, iyya* for the comparative and *iṭṭha, issika* for the superlative. The final consonant is generally dropped, as

pāpa—pāpiya, pāpiyya—pāpiṭṭha, pāpissika.

These adjectives are declined like *putta, kaññā* and *gharaṁ*.

Adjectives denoting possession and ending *vā, mā, vī* drop these suffixes before iya, iyya, iṭṭha, issika, as,

gunavā — guṇiya — guṇiṭṭha
satimā — satiyya — satiṭṭha
medhāvī — medhiya— medhiṭṭha

ADJECTIVES OF POSSESSION.

In forming these, *va* is added to bases in *a* and *ma* to bases in *i u*, *e.g.*, dhanavā, cakkhumā. The stem of these suffixes ends in *vat* or *vant*, *mat* or *mant*. Hence their declension and formation of the feminine is the same as the present participle active (see Lesson XIII.) *e.g.*

dhanavā puriso—a rich man
dhanavatī kaññā—a rich girl

dhanavantassa (*or* dhanavato) purisassa (*gen.*)
dhanavatiyaṁ kaññāyaṁ (*loc fem.*)

vī which denotes possession like vā, mā is added to nouns, while *āvī* is added to roots, as,

medhāvī—having wisdom
√pass—passāvī, seeing

They are declined like nouns in ī (*mas.* and *fem.*) and i (*neu*).

IRREGULAR COMPARISON OF ADJECTIVES.

Positive.	*Comparative.*	*Superlative.*
appa, few yuva, young	kaṇiya	kaṇiṭṭha
vuḍḍha, old	jeyya	jeṭṭha
pasattha, excellent	seyya	seṭṭha
garu, heavy	gariya	gariṭṭha
bāḷha, strong	sādhiya	sādhiṭṭha

NOTE:—The *ablative* is mostly used in comparison, as

So mayā pāpataro—he is more wicked than I am.

The three kinds of the Aorist.

(1) the *radical* aorist, formed by adding the aorist tense endings to the root, *e.g.*, √as, to be, *singular*, āsiṁ, āsi, āsi, *plural* āsimha, āsittha, āsiṁsu. Note that there is present the augment *a* (Lesson XI) a+as+iṁ=āsiṁ etc.

(2) the *stem* aorist, formed by adding the aorist endings to the base or stem, as, √pā—*singular* piviṁ, pivi, pivi—*plural*, pivimha, pivittha, piviṁsu. (base *piv.*)

(3) the *sigmatic* aorist, formed by inserting an *s* between the radical vowel or the vowel of the base and the aorist endings. These endings with *s* are usually added to roots ending in a vowel, the *s* serving to join the radical vowel to the aorist endings. *e.g*, √cur—*singular* coresiṁ, coresi, coresi, *plural* coresimha, coresittha, coresuṁ or coresiṁsu.

Translations :—1. Te maṁ dukkhā mocessanti. 2. So kaññaṁ taṇḍulaṁ pācesi. 3. Amacco tassa puttassa gāmaṁ dāpesi. 4. Te tayo purisā amhe bhattaṁ bhuñjāpesuṁ. 5. Cattāro puttā dve purise ekaṁ sīhaṁ māressanti. 6. Sace te mama dve sahāyā (*m. friend*) nāgaccheyyuṁ ahaṁ tehi saha gantuṁ na sakkuṇissāmi. 7. Cattāro corā ekissā guhāyaṁ (*f. cave*) mahantaṁ bhaṇḍaṁ nidahiṁsu (√dhā, to *hide*.) 8. Pakkosāhi (√kus to call) dasa purise. 9. Yadā mama pita āgacchāyya tadā maṁ pakkoseyya. 10. So cattāri sātakāni vikkiṇi.

1. We shall be led to the town 2. I was seen running after the man. 3. Make him conquer the country. 4. Sit down and make him play with the deer. 5. Four men and five girls kill the lion. 6. If you call me, I will go with you. 7. He was a very strong man. 8. They were my best friends. 9. The girl was older than the boy 10. Twenty thieves stole all my treasure.

Lesson XX.

FUTURE PASSIVE PARTICIPLE.

This participle is formed by the signs *tabba*, *anīya*, *ya*.

(*a*) Tabba is added (1) directly to roots ending in a vowel, as,

√hā—hātabba ; √dā—dātabba

The radical vowels i, ī are changed to *e*, as,

√nī—nettabba, √ji—jetabba.

Roots in u, ū form the *f.p.p.* from the base, as,

√bhū—bhavitabba, √cu—cavitabba. But √su—sotabba.

(2) Tabba may be joined to the root by means of 'i', as,

√pac—pacitabba, √pucch—pucchitabba.

(3) Tabba may be assimilated to the final consonant of the root according to the assimilation of *t* (Lesson XV) as,

√gam—gantabba : √labh—laddhabba.

NOTE :—Here again we have the three general rules of attaching the suffix to the root (directly, by means of 'i' and by assimilation) in common with other suffixes as the *p.p.p.*, the infinitive and the gerund (*which see*) because all these suffixes begin with 't'

(*b*) anīya may be added either to a root or a base, as,

√pac—pacanīya ; √bhū—bhavanīya ; √kar—karaṇīya

Note in the last example that the 'n' is dotted owing to the influence of the preceding r

(*c*) ya may be added

(1) directly to a root ending in a vowel, as,

√pā—peyya ; √dā—deyya ; √nī—neyya ; √ji—jeyya

(Note the form *eyya*)

(2) by means of 'i', as, √kar—kāriya ; √bhar—bhāriya.

(Note the long ā).

(3) by assimilation according to the rules of *ya* assimilation [Lesson VIII (*b*)] as, √khād—khajja : √bhuj—bhojja.

But √bhū+ya=bhavya=bhavva=bhabba (vv=bb.)

NOTE :—Here again the three general rules of passive formation are applicable to the *f.p.p.* The *f.p.p.* is also called the *participle of necessity* or *potential participle*, as it denotes *suitability* or *fitness* and is translated by "ought to be," "fit to be."

F. P. P. in the neuter form may be used as nouns (like the P. P. P.) *e.g.*, bhojjaṁ, khādanīyam—food, estables.

Reflexive Pronouns.

Attā—self, own.

	Singular	*Plural*
Nom.	Attā	Attāno
Gen. Dat.	Attano	Attānaṁ
Acc.	Attānaṁ	Attāno
Ins. Abl.	Attanā	Attanehi
Loc.	Attani	Attanesu

e.g., So attano gharaṁ gacchati—he goes to his own house.

NOTE:—The singular forms may be used idiomatically for the plural, especially the genitive singular, as,

Te attano gharāni gacchanti—they went to their own houses. *Sayaṁ* and *sāmaṁ* which are indeclinable are also reflexive pronouns, *e.g.*, So sāmaṁ karoti—he does it himself. Te sayaṁ karonti—they do it themselves.

Translations:—1. Dānaṁ dātabbaṁ silaṁ rakkhitabbaṁ 2. Te bhikkhavo kusalakammaṁ karaṇīyā. 3. Tumhe mama gharaṁ āgantvā bhojanīyaṁ bhuñjitvā vasitabbā. 4. So puriso etaṁ amaccaṁ bhattaṁ pāceyya. 5. Attā attano sāmiko (*lord*) bhavati. 6. Eso maggo (*road*) na gantabbo. 7. Taṁ bhattaṁ na khādanīyaṁ. 8. Etaṁ khīraṁ na pivitabbaṁ. 9. Taṁ na me dātabbaṁ. 10. So taṇḍulo puna (*again*) pacitabbo.

1. They themselves ate the food. 2. The girl herself struck me on the head. 3. Those men and these women ought to give food to those three elephants. 4. We shall make those men kill that lion. 5. I obtained my medicine from that king's daughter. 6. Make him lie down on the raft of that man. 7. You ought to salute the king. 8. They should come to my presence and ask me a question. 9. They sat on their own seats. 10. You have no need of my elephant.

Lesson XXI.

CAUSAL PASSIVE.

This is formed by adding *ya* to the causal base: the final *e* of the causal base is dropped and replaced by, i *e.g.*,

√pac—pāceti (*causal*)—pācīyati (*causal passive*) is caused to cook. √bhuj—bhojeti—bhojīyati—is caused to eat.

FUTURE PARTICIPLE.

This is formed by adding the present participle signs *anta* (active) and *māna* or *āna* (reflexive) to the future base, *e.g.*

	mas.	*fem.*	*neu.*
Act	pacissaṁ	pacissatī	pacissaṁ
	pacissanto	pacissantī	pacissantaṁ
Ref.	pacissamāno	pacissamānā	pacissamānaṁ
	pacissāno	pacissānā	pacissānaṁ

These are the same as the corresponding present participles in use and in declension. They of course have the future meaning, *viz.*, "while I shall be cooking."

NOTE:—Vaṭṭati is used with the instrumentive in the sense of *right, proper, fit, e.g.*, mayā taṁ gharaṁ gantuṁ vaṭṭati—It is proper for me to go to that house. The genitive may sometimes be used.

Sakka: is used with the instrumentive in the sense of *able, possible, e.g*, māyā taṁ gharaṁ gantuṁ na sakkā—It is not possible for me to go to that house.

The verb to be √hū (*homi, hosi, hoti, etc.*) is used to express possession, the possessor being put in the genitive, as,

Tassa puttā honti—he has sons.

Mayā ekā dhītā hoti—I have a daughter.

In practice the singular form *hoti* is usually used for the plural. Thus, Tassa puttā hoti.

Translations:—1. Te nagaraṁ carissamānā tassa gharaṁ gacchissanti. 2. So kammaṁ karissantaṁ taṁ purisaṁ vadhissati. 3. Amaccā pabbatassa samīpe tiṭṭhantāni gharāni āgacchanti. 4. Sā attano gharaṁ āgatā. 5. Pāpāni kammāni etehi purisehi katāni. 6. Tena dārakena pañhaṁ pucchituṁ na sakkā. 7. Aññesaṁ nidhiṁ coretuṁ na vaṭṭati. 8 Tassā kaññāya bhattaṁ laddhuṁ sakkā. 9 Tumhehi taṁ rājānaṁ passituṁ na vaṭṭati. 10. Etehi purisehi deviṁ passituṁ na sakkā.

1. The country has been conquered by those two kings. 2. The elephant has been brought by me from his house. 3. He has been killed by the man running after me. 4. When the house is given (*use the fut. part.*) to me by the girl, I shall live there. 5. If the raft is broken, call the owner. 6. It is proper for you to do good acts. 7. I am not able to give him food. 8. These men do not wish to hear the talk of these girls. 9. The ministers will not be able to reach the town. 10. The boy is not able to drink this water.

Lesson XXII.

GENITIVE AND LOCATIVE ABSOLUTE.

When a noun or pronoun in the gen. or loc. is used with a participle in the same case, the construction is called Genitive Absolute Construction or Locative Absolute Construction. The participle thus construed may be either present (act. and ref.) or passive perfect. The construction is translated by "while——" "when——", as, Tassa nagaraṁ gacchantassa (*or* gacchamānassa) ahaṁ taṁ vadhiṁ—as he was going to town I killed him.

or Tasmiṁ nagaraṁ gacchante ahaṁ taṁ vadhiṁ. With the *p.p.p.* the action shows completion, as Tasmiṁ nagaraṁ gate ahaṁ taṁ vadhiṁ—When he got to town I killed him.

NARRATION.

The sign *ti* short of *iti* is used after words of *saying, telling, thinking, naming* and such verbs to express direct narration or for the purpose of quotation. It is very often used with *āha* (3rd perfect of √ah), "he said" and āhaṁsu—" they said."

(*a*) The last vowel of a quotation must be long; if short must be lengthened. as, satthā "anāgate Buddho bhavissatī" ti vyākarosi—The teacher foretold "In future the the Buddha will arise."

Note.—The reason of the lengthening of the last vowel is this. The 'i' of *iti* being dropped, the last vowel is lengthened by way of compensation.

(*b*) Niggahīta is changed to '*n*' before *ti*, as, "Maranantaṁ hi jivitan" ti āha.—He said "Life indeed ends in death."

PRESENT.

√as- to be.

	Singular	*Plural.*
1.	Asmi, amhi	Asma, amha.
2.	Asi	Attha.
3.	Atthi	Santi.

Note.—*Santi* is formed by metathesis or interchange of letters. Thus, √as + nti (3rd pl.) would be asnti. Now, three consonants are not allowed to come together and asnti=santi by changing *as* into *sa*.

AORIST.

āsiṁ	āsimha.
āsi	āsittha.
si	āsuṁ, āsiṁsu.

Note.—It is this aorist that is used in the sigmatic aorist thus, *agamāsi*, etc.

OPTATIVE.

Assaṁ	Assāma.
Assa	Assatha.
Assa, siyā	Assu, siyuṁ.

IMPERATIVE.

Asmi, amhi	Asma, amha.
Ahi	Attha.
Atthu	Santu.

Pres. part.—Santa, samāna (*mas*) santī, satī, samānā (*f*).

Note.—Santa is used as an adjective meaning *good*, as, santo puriso—a good man. As a noun it means *the good* and is declined after the special declension of the present part active (Lesson XIII.)

Sato, gen. sing.; *sati*, loc. sing.; *sataṁ*, gen. pl.; *sabbhi* ins. abl. pl., *e.g.*, Sabbhi kusalaṁ kataṁ—merit is done by the good.

The initial vowel of the different forms of √as is affected by sandhi, as,

Ko 'si (=asi)—who art thou?
M 'āsi=me āsi—It was mine.

N.B.—*Atthi* like hoti is used idiomatically for the singular and plural to express possession, as,

Puttā mayhaṁ atthi—I have sons.

Translations:—1. "Ko si tvan" ti pucchati. 2. "So puriso mama sāmiko hotu" ti yācati. 3. Mātāpitaro attano dhītaraṁ "sujātā" ti nāmaṁ akaṁsu (*named*). 4. Te amaccā "Tumhehi kusalaṁ katan" ti āhaṁsu. 5. Kaññā "kin te etena sukhenā" ti pucchiṁsu. 6. Te maṁ tasmā dukkhā ca maraṇā mocessanti. 7. So taṁ bhattaṁ bhojesi. 8. Rājā tassa senāpatissa ekaṁ nagaraṁ dāpesi.

9. Te maṁ bhattaṁ bhuñjāpesuṁ. 10. Ahaṁ purise hatthiṁ māressāmi.

1. When he has cooked the rice, I will eat it. 2. Tell him, "you are very foolish." 3. She said, "If I get him, I shall live." 4. Who calls me? 5. "It is impossible for me to do it," they said. 6. The man said, "we are wise." 7. She said, "if I do not get it, I shall die." 8. The parents told their sons and daughters "you are very clever." 9. He said, "I know the queen's friend" 10. The girls said, "that work has not been done by you but by us."

Lesson XXIII.

INDECLINABLE WORDS.

Adverbs.

Ajja—to-day.
Ativiya—very, exceedingly.
Attha, atra—there
Atha—then, moreover
Antara—within.
Aparabhāge—subsequently
Api (pi)—even, though, perhaps
Appeva (api+eva)—perhaps
Ito—hence, from here
Idāni—now
Idha—here
Ettha—here
Eva (va)—as, like, even
Evaṁ—this
Kathaṁ—how?
Kadā—when?
Kadāci—sometimes
Kahaṁ, kattha—where?

Ciraṁ, cirassa—for a long time.
Tato—thence, from there.
Tatra, tattha—there.
Tathā—like that.
Tadā—then.
Tahiṁ—there.
Tāva, tavatā—so long, till then.
Divā—by day.
Nanu—is it not?
Nāma—namely, by name.
Nūna—surely, why not?
No—not
Pāto—early.
Puna—again
Punappunaṁ—again and again.
Pubbe, Pure—formerly

Kiṁ—why ?	Bahi—outside
Kuto—whence? from where?	Musā—falsely.
Kuhiṁ—where ?	Yato—whence.
Kuhiñci, kuhiñcanaṁ—anywhere	Yeva—eva, va.
	Rattiṁ—at night.
Kho—indeed	Viya—like, as if
	Sadā—always.
	Samantā—around, on all sides.
	Sammā—well, thoroughly.
	Sāyaṁ—in the evening.
	Hi—indeed. for
	Hiyyo—Yesterday.

The acc., gen., ins., abl. and loc. of some words are used as adverbs, *e.g.*,

(*a*) So *divasam* uyyāne vicari—He walked about in the garden for the whole day.

(*b*) So nadiṁ *jalatthaṁ* or *jalatthaya* gacchati—He goes to the river for water. Hence we have also *tadattham*—on that account, *kimatthaṁ*, why ? for what purpose ?

(*c*) So *vegena* dhāvati—he runs with speed.

(*d*) Yodhā nagaraṁ *samantato* parikkhipesuṁ—the warriors completely surrounded the town.

(*e*) *Atite* eko rāja vasi—long ago there lived a king

PROHIBITIVE PARTICIPLE.

Ma used with the aorist becomes prohibitive in sense, *e.g.*, mā akāsi—do not do.—Mā bhāyi—do not fear.

Mā may also be construed with the imperative, as, *mā gacchantu*—let them not go.

Note :—Some gerunds in *ya* are also used adverbially, *e.g.*,

(*a*) Ito *paṭṭhāya* mā taṁ akāsi—*Fron* this time, do not do it, (with the ablative) (*b*) Taṁ nagaraṁ *nissaya* eko rukkho hoti—*Near* (or *depending on*) that town is a tree (with the accusative).

(*c*) Satthā ekaṁ kaññaṁ *arabbha* (or *sandhaya*) taṁ vatthuṁ bhāsati.—The teacher tells that story *in connection* with (or *in relation to, concerning*) a girl. . . .

Translations :—1. Kuto āgacchati ? 2. Kuhiṁ gacchasi? 3. Kadā bhāsissasi ? 4. Kahaṁ vasasi ? 5. Aparabhāge so puriso mari. 6. Cando (*m. moon*) rattiṁ dippati (√dip, *to shine*). 7. Suriyo divā dippati. 8. Kathaṁ taṁ coraṁ ganhissāma ? 9. Evaṁ me sutaṁ. 10. Ajja mama gharaṁ mā gami.

1. Why do you do bad deeds ? 2. Where will you drink water ? 3. Ask him, "where do you live ?" 4. Do not go to his house tomorrow. 5. Today you must die. 6. You do not know anything concerning that man. 7. For what purpose has he run after the girl ? 8. He ran after the girl for the purpose of asking her name. 9. He slept the whole day 10. Long ago, there lived a banker with his wife.

Lesson XXIV.

INTERROGATION.

Besides the interrogative adverbs and pronouns, there are particles used in asking a question, *viz., api, nu.*

(*a*) Api as a sign of interrogation stands first in the sentence, as, Api dāraka amhākaṁ mātaraṁ jānāsi—do you, boy, know our mother ?

(*b*) Nu is generally followed by an indeclinable *kho*, as, Koci nu kho upaddavo hoti—is there any danger ?

Nu by itself is less common, as Sahāyā nu te atthi—Have you friends ?

(*c*) These two may be joined together for the sake of emphasis, as,

Api nu kho upaddavo hoti—Is there really any danger? Interrogation is also expressed by placing the verb first in the sentence, as, Gacchasi nagaraṁ—dost thou go to town?

Note:—When turning an affirmative sentence into an interrogative sentence *nu* generally comes second in the sentence, as,

Tvaṁ nu yodho—art thou a warrior?

NOTES ON *Ca* AND *Kāma*.

(*a*) When nominatives of different persons are connected by *ca* the verb takes the plural person of the last of them, as, So ca ahaṁ gacchāma—He and I go.

(*b*) Kāma is used as a suffix to the infinitive in the sense "desire." The niggahīta of the infinitive is invariably dropped, as, Sā maṁ passitukāmā—she desires to see me.

SUFFIXES.

Ahaṁ—*day*, as, ekāhaṁ, one day; dvīhaṁ, two days.

Ādi—*et cetera*, as sunakhahatthimigādayo (*pl*), dogs, elephants, deer, *et cetera*.

Ika—*belonging to, connected with*, as nāvika, sailor.

Ka—*agent, diminutive*, as, kāraka, doer; luddaka, little hunter.

Kāra—*making*, as bhattakāra, food-maker, cook.

Khattuṁ—*number of times*, as, tikkhattuṁ, thrice.

Ga, gū (*from* √*gam*)—*going*, as urago, going on the belly, *i.e.*, snake; pāragū, gone across, *i.e.*, accomplished.

Ja (√jā) *arising from*, as aṇḍaja, produced from an egg.

Ji (√*ji*)—*victorious*, Māraji, conquering of Māra.

Tama, Tara }—*Degrees of comparision*. See (Lesson XIX.)

Tā—*feminine abstract*, as, bālatā, folly.

Ttaṁ—*state*, as, matattaṁ, state of having died.

Dā, dāni—*time*, as, tadā, then; idāni, now.

Di—*like*, as, tādi, like that, such.
Disa—*like* as, mādisa, like me, tādisa, like that.
Dhā—*division*, as, dvidhā, divided into two.
Naṁ—*action*, as, gacchanaṁ, the act of going; dassanaṁ, the seeing, showing, appearance.
Nā (f)—*action*, as, desanā, the showing, instruction.
Bhāva—*state*, as, corabhāva, state of being a thief.
Mattaṁ—*extent, measure*, as, Yugamattaṁ, distance of a yuga.
Manta, mā / Vā, vantā } *possession*. (See Lesson XIX.)
Maya—*made of*, as, lohamaya, made of iron.
Yaṁ—*neuter abstract*, as, bālyaṁ, folly; paṇḍiccaṁ (paṇḍita+yaṁ), scholarship.
Sadisa—*like*, as suvaṇṇasadisa, like gold.

Note:—Suffixes like *ja, ji, ga, gu*, above, which are roots used as suffixes are called *Kvi* suffixes.

SANDHI (*contd.* from Lesson V.)

(*a*) e, o may be changed into their semivowels, *y*, *v* before a dis-similar vowel, as,

Te+atthu=tyatthu; me+ahaṁ=myāhaṁ (note *ā*) kho+assa=khvassa.

(*b*) dhi followed by a dis-similar vowel becomes *jjh*, as, adhi+āvasati=ajjhāvasati.

(*c*) Sometimes a consonant is inserted or *revived* from its original form between two vowels for the sake of euphony, as,

D.—tāva eva=tāva*d* eva.
M.—añña añña=añña*m*añña,
V.—so uṭṭhāti=so *v*uṭṭhāti.
Y.—na idaṁ=na *y*idaṁ.
R.—puna eva=puna*r* eva.

(*d*) A consonant coming after a single short vowel may be doubled, as, pa+kamo=pakkamo.

Note:—If the preceding vowel is long, the following consonant may be doubled provided the long vowel is shortened (because a long vowel is not generally allowed in front of a double consonant), as,

parā + kamo = parakkamo.

(*e*) In doubling a consonant aspirate, its non-aspirate is used in reduplication, as, ni + khipati = nikkhipati.

(*f*) ṁ followed by a vowel is changed to *m*
as, evaṁ āha = evamāha.

But note this change : —

taṁ eva = tameva = tam yeva (insertion of y) = taññeva.

Hence ṁ + y = ññ.

(*g*) ṁ followed by h may become ñ, as, taṁ hi = tañhi

(*h*) ṁ of the gen. pl., loc. sing. and the inf., may sometimes be dropped, as,

Buddhāna sāsanaṁ = Buddhānaṁ sāsanaṁ
Tasminagare = tasmiṁ nagare
Passitukāmo = passituṁ kāmo

Translations:—1. Te corā aññamaññaṁ paharanti. 2. Ete purisā attanehi gantuṁ na sakkā. 3. Ācariyo (*teacher*) sisse (*pupil m.*) sippāni (*art*) sikkhāpessati. 4. Koci nu taṁ dārakaṁ rukkhaṁ dassetvā tassa phalāni corāpesi. 5. Ahaṁ tisso itthī saccaṁ (*n.* truth) jānāpesiṁ. 6, Sā tumhe maraṇā mocessati. 7. Amhākaṁ pitā te manusse bhojetuṁ maṁ gacchāpeti. 8. Ko tumhe imasmiṁ gharasmiṁ vasāpeti. 9. So ca ahan taṁ sikkhāma. 10. Añño rājā etaṁ raṭṭhaṁ parājessati.

1. How did you do it? 2. Where did you see my father yesterday? 3. He died early in the morning. 4. On this side of the river you will see her lying down. 5. Sometimes he does evil deeds. 6. They always tell lies. 7. Are you coming with me. 8. He and I will sell this cart. 9. Bring me some food. 10. Is he not a fool?

Lesson XXV.

SĀMASA (COMPOUND WORDS).

This may be divided into six kinds., *viz.*

(1) Dvanda or aggregative
(2) Tappurisa or case-dependent
(3) Kammadhāraya or descriptive
(4) Digu or numeral
(5) Abyayibhāva or adverbial
(6) Bahubbihi or relative

Note:—In forming compound words, the case-endings of all members except the last are dropped *i.e.*, the base is used except in the last member. Generally bases in i and u are placed first.

(1) In Dvanda the members may be separated by *ca*, as,

Devamanussā (devā ca manussā ca), gods and men.

Candimasuriyā (candimā ca suriyo ca), the sun and the moon.

Note that these examples are in the plural from, each member being considered *separately* Such forms are called *Itaritara*. Some dvanda compounds may be put in the neuter singular form, being considered *collectively* Such forms are then called *Samāhāra*, *e.g.*,

Hatthiassaṁ (hatthino ca assā ca)—elephants and horses.

Jarāmaraṇaṁ, old age and death.

(2) In Tappurisa the first member *determines* the case of the last member. The first member may therfore be in any case except the nom. and voc., *e.g.*,

(*a*) Kumbhakāro=kumbhaṁ karo, a pot-maker (in the acc. relation)

(*b*) Urago=urena go, going by the breast, snake (in the inst. relation.)

(*c*) Rājaputta=rañño putta, kings's son (in the gen. relation.)

(*d*) Buddhadeyyaṁ = Buddhassa deyyaṁ, gift for the Buddha (in the dat. relation.)

NOTE—The inf. with *kāma* as suffix is considered to be a Tappurisa in the dat. relation, as, gantukāmo = gantuṁ kāmo.

(*e*) Corabhayaṁ = corasmā bhayaṁ, fear from a thief (in the abl. relation.)

(*f*) Vanacaro = vane caro, a forester (in the loc. relation.)

NOTE.—Sometimes the first member may be put last, as, rājahaṁso = haṁsānaṁ rājā, king of swans.

Sometimes the case-ending of the first member is not dropped. Hence the name *alutta tappurisa*, as,

Parassapadaṁ -- word for word—Active Voice (parassa padaṁ.)

Manasikāro — doing in the mind, *i.e.*, attention (manasi kāro.)

(3) In Kammadhāraya the first member is an adjective qualifying the last, as, mahāpuriso—a great man.

NOTE.--The qualifying member may come last, as, purisuttamo = uttamo puriso, the greatest man.

Words with the negative sign *a* or *an* are considered as kammadhāraya, as,

Anariyo—ignoble.

Nouns in apposition are also considered as kammadhāraya as,

Magadhabhāsā—the language of Magadha.

(4) In Digu the first member is a numeral. Like the Dvanda the Digu may be considered collectively (*samāhāra*) as, tiratanaṁ—the Three Jewels or individually (a samāhāra) as, catudisā—the four cardinal points.

(5) In Abyayibhāva the first member is an indeclinable, as,

Yathāsukhaṁ—at pleasure.

(6) When any of the above five compounds is used as an adjective qualifying a noun or pronoun (expressed or understood), it becomes Bahubbīhi, *e.g.*

Buddhabhāsito dhammo—the Law spoken by the Buddha. Here Buddhabhāsito is in itself a tappurisa in the *inst. relation*, but because it qualifies *dhammo* becomes Bahubbihi.

Pañcasatāni sakaṭāni—five hundred carts. Here also pañcasatāni is a Digu, but qualifying sakaṭāni becomes Bahubbīhi.

Saphalo rukkho—a tree with fruits. This is Abyayibhāva used as Bahubbıhi.

In explaining a long compound it is advisable to begin from the last member and explain backwards. Thus,

Nagaraṁ vividhasamaṇabrāhmaṇasabhājanasaṅghaṭitaṁ.

= nagaraṁ vividhasamaṇabrāhmaṇasabhājanehi—saṅghaṭitaṁ (Tappurisa in the inst. relation).

= nagaraṁ vividhasamaṇabrāhmaṇānaṁ—sabhājanehi saṅghaṭıtaṁ (Tappurisa in the gen relation)

=nagaraṁ vividhasamaṇānañ *ca* brāhmaṇānaṁ sabhājanehi saṅghaṭitaṁ. (Dvandva)

= nagaram vividhānaṁ samaṇānañ ca vividhānaṁ brahmaṇānaṁ sabhājanehi saṅghaṭitaṁ (kammadhāraya)

And as the whole compound qualifies *nagaraṁ* it is Bahubbihi. The meaning is—the town which resounds with the welcoming shouts of various samaṇas and Brāhmaṇas.

Expletives and Intensitives.

Atha - *and, then, moreover*, as Ath'eko luddo taṁ migaṁ Vadhi - then one hunter killed that deer.

Api (pi)—*also, even, though*, as evaṁ sante pi,—though being so.

Note: *pi* coming directly after a pres. or p.p. participle or a gerund means *although*, as, Taṁ purisaṁ oloketvā pi na sañjānāmi—Though I look at that man I do not recognize him.

Eva, yeva—*even, just only*, as, Tasmiṁ ṭhāne yeva mari—Even at that place he died.

Kho—*indeed*, as, Sā kho paṇḍitā—she is indeed clever

Nāma—*namely*, as Mahājanako nāma rājā ahosi—there was a king by name Mahājanaka.

Va—is short for either eva (*which see*) or of *iva, like*, as So corova dhāvati—he runs like a thief.

Note: *Va* coming directly after a p p p. or a gerund means *as soon as, e.g*,

So nagaram pavisitvā va gahito—as soon as he entered the town, he was caught.

Tam vacanam sutvā va kujjhi—as soon as he heard that word, he became angry.

Hi—*for, indeed, therefore*, as, so hi paṇḍito—for he is clever.

Perfect Participle Active.

This is formed by adding *vā* to the p.p.p., as,

p.pp.—pacita; p.p.a—pacitavā.

These participles are declined like the pres. part., *nom*. pacitavā, *fem*-pacitavatī, pacitavantī, *neu*-pacitavantam, pacitavaṁ, The declension is thus in common with that of the possessives in *vā, mā* and the adj *mahā* great). Mahā thus has two stems *mahat and mahant* like the two stems of the pres part.

Note: The *vā* may be changed to *vī* provided the preceding vowel is lengthened, as, pacitavā=pacitāvī. This form is declined like nouns in ī, *i.e.*, sakkhī in the mas. (p. 10) nadī in the fem. (p. 14) and

Translations:—1. Candasuriyā sobhanti 2. Buddhasāsanaṁ sevati. 3. So yathāsukhaṁ vasati. 4. Ācariyo maṁ catusaccaṁ sikkhāpeti. 5. Te pāragaṅgaṁ nassiṁsu (√nas—to *perish*). 6. Pacitabhattaṁ detha. 7. Pitupesitadūtavacanaṁ suṇātha 8. Luddapaharitamigo mari. 9. Kīḷantadārakā niddāyanti. 10 Hatthachinno puriso nirupakāro.

Form into compounds:—1. The girl's father. 2. The boy's mother. 3. Happiness and suffering. 4. A bird and a monkey. 5. The boy who is eating food. 6. The man seated on the tree. 7. Fear of death. 8. Thieves caught by men. 9. A mother's advice. 10. Hand and foot.

Lesson XXVI.

DENOMINATIVE VERBS.

These are so called because they are formed from *noun-stems* by adding certain suffixes. They are generally translated by (*a*) "to act like, to wish to be like;" (*b*) "to desire," "to wish for;" (c) "to make use of, to change into" that which is expressed by the noun.

The suffixes mostly used are *e*, *aya*, *āya*, *iya*, *īya* and *āpe*.

Noun-Stem.	*Denominative verb.*
e.g.	
pabbata, mountain	pabbatāyati, to act like a mountain
arañña, forest	araññiyati, to behave as in a forest.
gaṇa, a following	gaṇayati, to wish for a following.

samodhāna, connection — samodhāneti, to connect, join.

sukha, happiness — sukhāpeti, to make happy.

Note: Denominatives may also be formed from adjectives and adverbs, as,

aṭṭa, hurt—aṭṭayati, to hurt.
daḷha, firm—daḷhayati, to make firm.

DESIDERATIVE VERBS.

These verbs are formed by reduplicating the root and adding the suffix *sa*. They express desire or wish.

Root	*Desid. base*	*Desid. verb*
√su, to hear	sussusa	sussusati, desires to hear, listens.
√bhuj, to eat	bubhukkha (*j*+*s*=*kkh*).	bubhukkhati, to wish to eat, feel hungry.

INTENSIVE VERBS.

These express the intensification or frequent repetition of the action denoted by the root. The base is formed by reduplicating the root, *e.g.*

√kam, to go—caṅkamati, to walk to and fro.
√cal, to shake, move—cañcalati, to move up and down, to tremble, shake.

MISCELLANEOUS VERBS.

The following forms may be useful to the student :—

(*a*) √kar, to make, do.

AORIST.

	Singular.	*Plural.*
1.	Akāsiṁ	Akāsimhā
2.	Akāsi	Akāsittha
3.	Akāsi	Akāsuṁ, akaṁsu.

These forms are more widely used than the ordinary *karim*, *kari etc.*

(*b*) √dā, to give

AORIST.

1. Adāsiṁ	Adāsimhā
2. Adāsi	Adāsittha
3. Adasi	Adāsuṁ, adaṁsu.

FUTURE.

1. Dassāmi	Dassāma
2. Dassasi	Dassatha
3. Dassati	Dassanti

The usual forms would be *dalissāmi*, etc.

(*c*) √ṭhā, to stand—base *tiṭṭha*.

AORIST.

1. Aṭṭhāsiṁ	Aṭṭhāsimhā
2. Aṭṭhasi	Aṭṭhāsittha
3. Atthāsi	Aṭṭhaṁsu

FUTURE.

1. Thassāmi	Thassāma
2. Ṭhassasi	Ṭhassatha
3. Ṭhassati	Thassanti

The usual forms from the base would be *tiṭṭhissāmi* etc.

(*d*) √ñā—to know; base, jāna.

AORIST.

Singular.	*Plural.*
1. Jāniṁ	Jānimhā
2. Jāni	Jānittha
3. Jāni	Jāniṁsu
or	
1. Aññāsiṁ	Aññāsimhā
2. Aññāsi	Aññāsittha
3. Aññāsi	Aññāsiṁsu

(e) √ brū, to say.

AORIST.

1. Abraviṁ	Abravimhā
2. Abravi	Abravittha
3. Abravi	Abravuṁ, abraviṁsu

(f) √ vac, to speak.

AORIST.

1. Avacam	Avacamhā
2. Avaca	Avacattha
3. Avaca, avoca	Avacum, avocum.

GER.—vatvā.

(g) √ das, to see.

AORIST.

1. Addasaṁ	Addasamhā
2. Addasa	Addasatthā
3. Addasa	Addasuṁ

GER—disvā.

(h) √ hū, to be—base, ho.

AORIST.

1. Ahosiṁ	Ahosimhā.
2. Ahosi	Ahosittha.
3. Ahosi	Ahesuṁ.

FUTURE.

1. Hessāmi.	Hessāma.
2. Hessasi.	Hessatha.
3. Hessati.	Hessanti.

GER.—hutvā:

INF.—hotuṁ.

It will be noted that the sigmatic endings are usually added to the root.

DECLENSION OF NOUNS IN *o* OR *ae*

There are some nouns which end in *o* or *ae*. Their declension is on the lines of *pitū*, *rājā* though not exactly the same.

Mano—mind.

	Singular.	*Plural.*
Nom.	Mano.	Manā.
Gen. Dat.	Manaso, Manassa.	Manānaṁ.
Acc.	Mano, Manaṁ.	Mane.
Ins.	Manasā, Manena.	Manehi, Manebhi,
Abl.	Manasā, Manasmā, Manamhā, Manā.	(Manehi, Manebhi,)
Loc.	Manasi, Mane, Manasmiṁ, Manamhi.	Manesu.
Voc.	Mano, Mana.	Manā.

Nouns (like mano)—vaco, discourse; vayo, age; ceto, thought; yaso, fame, uro, breast; ojo, strength; tejo, power; tapo, heat; tamo, darkness, ayo, iron; siro, the head.

DECLENSION OF THE DEMONSTRATIVE Ayaṁ—this (SUBSTANTIVE AND PRONOUN).

Masculine.

	Singular.	*Plural.*
Nom.	Ayaṁ.	Ime.
Gen. Dat.	Assa, imassa.	Imesānaṁ, imesaṁ, esānaṁ, esaṁ.
Acc.	Imaṁ.	Ime.
Ins.	Anena, iminā.	Imehi, imebhi, ehi, ebhi.
Abl.	Asmā, imasmā, imamhā.	(Imehi, imebhi, ehi, ebhi.)
Loc.	Asmiṁ, imasmiṁ, imamhi.	Imesu, esu.

Feminine.

Nom.	Ayaṁ.	Imā, imāyo.

Gen. Dat.	Assāya, assā, imassāya, imissā, imāya.	Imāsānaṁ, imāsaṁ.
Acc.	Imaṁ.	Imā, imāyo.
Ins. Abl.	Imāya, assā, imissā.	Imāhi, imābhi.
Loc.	Assaṁ, imissaṁ, assā, imissā, imāyaṁ, imāya.	Imāsu.

Neuter.

Nom.	Idaṁ, imaṁ	Imāni.
Gen. Dat.	Imassa, assa.	Imesaṁ, imesānaṁ, esānaṁ, esaṁ.
Acc.	Idaṁ, imaṁ.	Imāni.
Ins.	Iminā, anena.	Imehi, imebhi, ehi, ebhi.
Abl.	Imasmā, amhā, asmā.	
Loc.	Imasmiṁ, asmiṁ, imamhi	Imesu, esu.

Translations :—1. Ācariyo attano sissehi saha samuddassa pāraṁ gantvā tumhākaṁ gāme (*m. village*) hessati. 2. Ahaṁ tava sisso hessāmi. 3. Mayaṁ sīhaṁ disvā cetiyassa pacchato aṭṭhāsimhā. 4. Purisā ca itthiyo ca pānīyaṁ pivituṁ nagarassa avidure nadiṁ yanti. 5. Rājā pāsādaṁ upasaṅkamitvā deviyā santike taṁ purisaṁ addasa. 6. Mama pitā attanā taṁ kammaṁ katvā muhuttaṁ (*awhile*) niddāyi. 7. Mā yena Bhagavā ten' upasaṅkāhi. 8. Gāmassa antare sīhā ahesuṁ. 9. Tvaṁ te manusse mama gharassa heṭṭhā passissasi. 10. Ayaṁ mama putto hessati.

1. There are trees on the top of that mountain. 2. The hunter went behind the deer and killed it with a javelin. 3. All of you should go into the presence of the king and ask this question. 4. He spoke to me " You must not do this deed again." 5. There will be two sons and three daughters to them. 6. I stood within the house, but she stood outside. 7. Are you not coming with me to see him? 8. Are they thirsty or hungry? 9. Is the moon far away from the sun or close to it? 10. I cannot tell you that.

Lesson XXVII.

DERIVATION.

This 'consists in tracing a Pali word to its root. For instance, Abhisambujjhissati = abhi (pref.) + saṁ (pref.) √budh—to know + ya (3rd cong.) + issati (3rd sing. future) Thus the root √budh is obtained.

Derivation is divided into *Kita* or primary, and *Taddhita* or secondary.

Kita derivation consists of suffixes and prefixes added directly to the root, as √khād + ya = khajja, eatable.

Taddhita derivation consists of suffixes added to the ase or stem, as, manussa, man + ttaṁ = mānussattaṁ—tate of being a man.

In taddhita derivation guṇa of the vowel in the first syllable usually takes place, *e.g.*, karuṇā, mercy + ika = kāruṇika, merciful.

It will thus be seen that almost all the inflections that have been given in the previous Lessons, such as the suffixes of the P.P.P., F.P.P. gerund, infinitive, the seven conjugations and other suffixes come under the kita derivation.

It is sufficient for the present purpose of this primer tha the student should know these suffixes well. He will have no difficulty in recognizing as kita derivatives any other suffixes he may meet with in the course of his reading.

Taddhita Derivatives: The following are the most common.

1. A—to form nouns and adjectives in the sense of
   (*a*) *patronymics* :—as Vāsiṭṭho, son of Vasiṭṭha
   (*b*) *belonging to* :—as, Māgadho, belonging to Magadha.

(*c*) *proficient in*:—as, nemittako, one who knows nimitta, omens.

2. Aka—*belonging to*:—manussaka, human,

3. Āna—*patronymics*:—as, Kaccāno, son of Kacca.

4. Āyana—*patronymics*:—as, Kaccāyana, son of Kacca.

5. Era—*patronymics*:—as, Vedhavero, son of Vidhava.

6. Eyya—(*a*) *state or nature*:—as, ālaseyyaṁ, state of being idle (alasa)

(*b*) *patronymics*:—as, māleyya, the gardener's son (mālī)

(*c*) a form of the F.P.P. (see p. 44).

7. I—*patronymics*:—as, Doni, son of Duna.

8. Ika—(*a*) *patronymics*:—as, Nádaputtiko, son of Nādaputta.

(*b*) *connected with, belonging to*:—as, bālisiko, connected with a hook (balisa), fisherman; Sāvatthiko, a resident of Sāvatthi; pādika, going on foot.

(*c*) *mixed with*:—as, telikaṁ, mixed with oil (tela)

(*d*) *proficient in*:—as, venayiko, a student of Vinaya

9. Ima—*direction in time or space*:—as, pacchima, western (pacchā)

10. Imā—*possession* (see p. 41).

11. In—*adjectival*. This is the stem of nouns, the nom-sing. of which ends in ī like sakkhī (p. 10)

12. Issika—*superlative* (p. 41).

13. Iya—*abstract*:—as, issariyaṁ, lordship (issara)

14. Iya, īya—F.P.P. (p. 44).

15. Ī—*ordinal numbers*:—as, ekādasī—the eleventh.

16. Ka—(*a*) *collection*:—as, mānussakaṁ, a group of men.

(*b*) *diminutive*:—as, luddako, a young hunter.

(*c*) Sometimes this adds nothing to the sense—as, Kumāraka, prince.

17. La—*abundant in, possessed of*:—as, vācala, talkative; bahula, abundant.

18. Ma—See *ima*. It also forms ordinals. (p. 39).

19. Mā—*possessive*:—see (p. 41).

20. Maya—*made of*:—as rajatamaya, made of silver.

21. Min=mī—*possessive*:—as, gomin, gomī, owner of cattle.

22 Ra (preceded by i, ā)—*adjectival*:—as, madhura, sweet (madhu); kammāra, worker (kamma).

23. So—*possessive*.—as, lomaso, hairy (loma)

24. Ta—*possessive*:—as, pabbata, mountain (pabba—joint) also P.P.P (see p. 29.]

25. Tama—*superlative* (p. 41).

26. Tara—*comparative* (p. 41).

27. Tā—(*a*) *fem. abstract*:—as, Saratā, essence (sāra) lahutā, lightness (lahu)

(*b*) *collection*:—as, gāmatā, collection of villages (gāma)

28. Tta—*state*.—as, buddhattaṁ—Buddhahood.

29. Tha—*ordinals* (p. 39).

30. Thaṁ—*pronominal adverbs of manner*:—as, kathaṁ. how?

31. Thā—manner:—as, tathā, like that.

32. Vā—*possessive*—p. 41.

33. Vin = Vī—*possessive* :—as, tapas + vī = tapassī austere; yasas + vī = yasassī, famons

34. Ya—***neuter abstract*** :—as, kosallaṁ, skill (kusala); paṇḍiccaṁ (paṇḍita + yaṁ) scholarship.

Tenses of the Reflexive Voice.

The tense terminations so far given belong to the active voice. Theoretically the difference between the active and the reflexive is this:

When the result of the action expressed by the verb accrues to another *other* than the agent, it is active; when it accrues to the agent it is reflexive: *e.g.*

pacati—he cooks (for somebody else.)

pacate—he cooks (for himself.)

But in practice this difference is not observed and active and reflexive may be taken to mean the same thing. All reflexive endings are not equally important; some are very seldom met with. But some are regularly used and the student should note them well. They are the present, future, optative and the imperative. The full table is here given:—

√pac—to cook. (reflexive voice).

Present.

Singular.	*Plural*
Pace	Pacamhe
Pacase	Pacavhe
Pacate	Pacare, pacante

Imperfect.

Apaciṁ	Apacāmhase, apacamhase
Apacase	Apacavhaṁ
Apacattha	Apacatthuṁ

IMPERATIVE.

Pace	Pacamāse
Pacassu	Pacavho
Pacataṁ	Pacantaṁ.

OPTATIVE.

Paceyyaṁ	Paceyyāmhe
Pacetho	Paceyyavho
Pacetha	Paceraṁ

AORIST.

Apaca	Apacimhe
Apacise	Apacivhaṁ
Apacā, apacū	Apacuṁ, apaciṁsu

PERFECT.

Papaci	Papacimhe
Papacittho	Papacivho
Papacittha	Papacire

FUTURE.

Pacissaṁ	Pacissāmhe
Pacissase	Pacissavhe
Pacissate	Pacissante

CONDITIONAL.

Apacissaṁ	Apacissāmhase
Apacissase	Apacissavhe
Apacissatha	Apacissiṁsu

Translations:—1 Navā (*new*) bhikkhuṇiyo therānaṁ (*m. monk*) bhikkhuṇīnañca pāde vandante. 2. Therā purā sīlavantiyo babhūvu. 3. Puññāvantassa dhītaro dhītimantiyo ca sīlavantiyo ca guṇavantiyo ca paññāvantiyo ca ahesuṁ. 4. Upāsikā (*f. disciple*) sabbāpi dhammacāriṇiyo ca sīlavantiyo ca siyuṁ. 5. Tassā deviyā ekā medhāvinī guṇavatī dhitā ahosi. 6. Guṇavā puriso tesaṁ gharaṁ gantvā bhattaṁ bhuñjitvā paccāgacchate. 7. Cakkhumā (*foreseeing*) Bhagavā sattānaṁ (*m. a being*) kusalatthāya sukhatthāya dhammaṁ desetvā yathāsukhaṁ vicari. 8. Atta-d-atthaṁ paratthena na parājeyya. 9. Sirimā cando rattiyaṁ sobhati. 10. Bhānumā (*brilliant*) suriyo divā ālokaṁ (*m. light*) deti.

1. A clever boy learns his own lessons. 2. A man who has many friends ought to possess much wealth. 3. Could you tell me when he went to Sāvatthi? 4. What good to thee, O fool, by doing bad actions? 5. Happy people (*m. jana. sing.*) do not die young (yuvā). 6. A strong man ought to do much work in the course of the day. 7. The wise teacher will instruct his diligent (viriyavā) pupils. 8. A talkative person will not be able to learn much. 9. The bird flew far away and dropped down (√pat.) dead. 10. Lions roam about at night in search of (*atthāya*) deer.

Lesson XXVIII.

SYNTĀX (KARAKA).

The order of a Pali sentence is subject, object and predicate, as, So bhattaṁ khādati—He eats food.

Attributes of the subject and the object come before them; adverbs come before the verb, as, Te purisā mahantaṁ siriṁ khippena labhiṁsu—those men obtained great glory quickly.

But adverbs of time always begin the sentence, as Tadā so mari—At that time he died.

Nominative :—This is used as in English, also in apposition and as titles as, Sakka devindo—Sakka, king of gods; Mahājanakajātaka—story of Mahājanaka.

Genitive:—Expresses (*a*) *possession* as, dāṛakassa kāyo—the boy's body.

(*b*) *Is used in a partitive sense*, purisānaṁ seṭṭho—best of men.

(*c*) Words expressing various degrees of feeling such as *hatred*, *love*, *envy*, *fear*, *honour*, *faith*, etc., are construed with the genitive, as,

Sā mama manapā (or amanapā), she is dear (or hateful)to me.

Sā mama piheti, she envies me.

Sabbe maraṇassa bhāyanti, all fear death.

Ahaṁ mahājanassa pūjito, I am honoured of the people.

So Buddhassa pasanno, he has faith in the Buddha (Loc, also may be used).

(*d*) To express *proficiency*:—Abhidhammassa kusalo, clever in Abhidhamma.

(*e*) With words of *longing*, *filling*, as,

So mama sarati, be remembers me (sentimentally).

So pāpassa pūrati, he is full of evil

Dative:—Expresses (*a*) purpose, as, niddāya paccāgacchi, he came back to sleep.

(*b*) Is construed with words of *praise*, *injury*, *approval*, *salutation*, *blessing*, *concealing*, etc., as, Sotthi te hotu, may you prosper.

Tassa sampaṭicchāmi, I agree with him.

Dārakassa rocate sakuṇo, the bird pleases the boy.

(*c*) With *alam*, fit, *attha*, purpose, *hita* benefit, *sukha*, happiness, as, Alaṁ coro corassa, a thief is a match for a thief.

So bhattassa atthāya gacchati, he goes for food.

Bhagavā devamanussānaṁ hitaya sukhāya dhammaṁ deseti, the Blessed One teaches the Law for the happiness and benefit of gods and men.

(*a*) Destination of one's movements is sometimes put in the dative, as, so maṁ rañño neti, he leads me to the king.

Accusative:—expresses, (*a*) object, So main paharati, he strikes me

(*b*) Verbs of motion govern the acc., as, So nagaraṁ gacchati, be goes to town.

(*c*) Verbs of ***choosing, naming, calling, asking, knowing, thinking*** & Co., govern two accusatives ;—as, So maṁ pañhaṁ pucchati, he asks me a question.

(*d*) The roots √vas, to live; √ṭhā, to stand ; √ si, to lie ; √pad, to step;√vis, to enter when preceded by certain prefixes govern the acc., as, Te gāmaṁ upavasanti, they live in the village ; Te mañcaṁ abhinisīdanti, they sit on the cot.

(*e*) Certain indeclinables govern the acc., as, Taṁ ṭhapetvā sabbe gacchare, excepting him they all went ; so abhito nagaraṁ vasati, he lives near the town.

(*f*) *Duration of time* :—divasaṁ kammaṁ karoti, he works the whole day.

(*g*) *Distance* :—yojanaṁ gacchati, be goes a yojana.

(*h*) *Adverbially* :—sīghaṁ dhāvati, he runs quickly.

Instrumentive :—expresses (*a*) ***agent*** or ***instrument***, as sotena saddaṁ suṇāti, one hears sounds by the ear.

(*b*) ***cause or reason***, as, vyādhinā marati, he dies on account of sickness.

(*c*) ***mode of conveyance***, as sakaṭena gacchati, he goes by cart.

(*d*) *market price*, as, kahapaṇena kiṇāti, he buys it for a coin.

(*e*) *Route*, as, dvārena gacchati, he goes out by the door.

(*f*) *Birth, origin, nature*, as, pakatiyā pāpakārī, an evil-doer by nature.

(*g*) *Occupation of time*, as, māsena sikkhati, he learns it in a month.

(*h*) *Companionship*, as, tena saddhim mā gacchi, do not go with him.

(i) *Uselessness, futility* as, kin te āgacchantena, what good is there by your coming.

(*j*) *With alaṁ*, fit, *attho*, need, as, alaṁ ambehi, enough of mangoes ; sakaṭena me attho, I want a cart.

(*k*) *Parts of the body as means of conveyance*, as, sisena bhaṇḍaṁ vahati, he carries the bundle on his head.

Ablative :—expresses (*a*) *Separation* and other ideas denoted by *from*, as, nagarasmā gacchanti, they go from the own.

(*b*) *Measure of length, breadth, or distance*, as, yojanaṁ āyāmato, a yojana in length.

(*c*) *Object from which something is to be avoided*, as, ambehi kāke rakkhati, he keeps crows away from the mangoes.

(*d*) *Motive*, as, guṇato taṁ pasaṁsanti, they praise him for his virtues.

(*e*) *origin*, as, corā bhayaṁ jāyati, fear arises from a thief.

(*f*) is construed with certain indeclinables, as, aññatra Bhagavatā añño ācariyo me n' atthi, besides the Blessed one, I have no other teacher.

Locative expresses (*a*) *time* or *place* in which something is done, as, gharasmiṁ niddāyati, he sleeps in the house; sāyaṇhasamaye, in the evening.

(*b*) *motive*, as, Hatthī dantesu haññate, the elephant is killed for his tusks.

(*c*) *excellence by comparison*, as, manussesu seṭṭho best among men.

Note that the gen. is also used as, manussānaṁ seṭṭho.

(*d*) is construed with words of *saluting*, *delighting*, *striking*, *kissing* etc., as, kusalasmiṁ ramati, he delights in merit; Bhikkhavo Bhagavate abhivādenti, the monks salute the Bhagavā.

(*e*) with *adhi*, superior, and *upa*, *inferior*, as, Adhi devesu Buddho, the Buddha is superior to the gods. Upa khāriyaṁ doṇo, a doṇa is less than a khārī.

(*f*) expresses *proximity*, as, nadiyaṁ kutī, a hut near the river.

(*g*) Loc. is often used for other cases, *e.g.*
tayi yuttaṁ, fit for thee (for the gen.)

pattesu piṇḍāya caranti, they go about for food with their bowls (for the inst.)

saṅghe dinnaṁ mahapphalaṁ, gifts to the clergy are very fruitful (for the dat.)

ambesu kāke rakkhanti, they keep the crows from the mangoes (for the abl.)

(*h*) *adverbially*, as, atīte, long ago.

Lesson XXIX.

SOME USEFUL PHRASES.

1. Atthaṁ gacchati—to come to a conclusion, to set (of the sun.)

2. Antaraṁ karoti—to seize the opportunity.
3. Abhayaṁ yācati—to ask for security of life.
4. Uraṁ dadāti—to put forth effort.
5. Etad ahosi—to think thus.
6. Evaṁ sante—it being so.
7. Kālaṁ karoti—to die.
8. Jaṅghāvihāraṁ anucaṅkamati—to take exercise.
9. Jīvikaṁ kappeti—to support oneself in life.
10. Jīvitakkhayaṁ pāpeti—to kill (*lit* to cause to get loss of life).
11. Niddaṁ okkamati—to sleep.
12. Nimittaṁ gaṇhāti—to fall in love with.
13. Rajjaṁ kāreti—to rule, govern.
14. Vāsaṁ kappeti—to dwell.
15. Sace te agaru—if you please.
16. Saṅgaraṁ moceti—to fulfil one's promise.
17. Saññaṁ dadāti—to give a sign.
18. Sīsaṁ karoti—to lay the head down on.
19. Sīhanādaṁ nadati—to shout in exultation (*lit* to shout the lion's shout)
20. Hatthagataṁ karoti—to take possession of (*lit* to make it come to one's hands)

EXPLANATION OF A SHORT TEXT.

Evaṁ me sutaṁ. Ekaṁ samayaṁ Bhagavā Sāvatthiyaṁ viharati Jetavane Anāthapiṇḍikassa ārāme. Atha kho aññatarā devatā abhikkantāya rattiyā abhikkantavaṇṇā kevalakappaṁ Jetavanaṁ obhāsetvā yena Bhagavā ten' upasaṅkami, upasaṅkamitvā Bhagavantaṁ abhivādetvā ekamantaṁ aṭṭhāsi. Ekamantaṁ ṭhitā kho sā devatā Bhagavantaṁ gāthāya ajjhabhāsi.

Evaṁ—indeclinble, *thus*,
me—inst. of *ahaṁ*, first person pronoun, *by me*.
sutaṁ—p.p.p. neuter of √su, to hear.
Ekaṁ—numeral, *one*, agreeing with *samayaṁ*..
samayaṁ—adverbial acc. cf samaya, *time*.
Bhagavā—nom. from bhaga, power+vā (possessive).
Sāvatthiyaṁ—loc. sing. of Sāvatthī (*f*) name of a town.

viharati—historical present (used for the past, quite commonly met with) of vi+√har, to live, 3rd sing.

Jetavane—loc. sing. of Jetavana=Jetassa vana (Tappurisa in the gen. relation) Jeta's park, in apposition with ārāme.

Anathāpiṇḍikassa—gen. sing. of Anāthapiṇḍika, name of a person, so called because he was the feeder (piṇḍika) of the needy (a-nātha).

ārāme—loc. sing of ārāma, monastery.
Atha—adverb, *then*
kho—expletive.

aññatarā—adj. a *certain* f agreeing with devatā, nom case.
devatā—nom fem. *fairy*.
abhikkantāya—loc. fem. of abhikkanta, p.p.p. of abhi+√kam, to pass + ta, agreeing with *rattiyā*.
rattiyā—loc. fem. of *ratti* night.

abhikkantavaṇṇā—Kammadhāraya compd. qualifying *devatā* becomes bahubbihi=abhikkanta (*p.p.p.* of abhi √kam. to be lovely+ta)+vaṇṇā, fem. nom used as adj qualifying *devatā*.

kevalakappaṁ—adj. qualifying Jetavanaṁ, acc. case.
obhāsetvā—ger.=o (ava, pref.)+√bhās, to shine +e (causal)+tvā.

yena—tena, correlative (inst.) denotes *direction* of place.

upasaṅkami—aor. 3rd sing. of upa+saṁ+√kaṁ, to go, step+i.

upasaṅkamitvā—ger. of the preceding.

Bhagavantaṁ—acc. of Bhagavā.

abhivādetvā—ger, abhi+√vad, to speak+e (caus.)+tvā

ekamantaṁ—Digu compd.=eka—m (euphonic)—antaṁ (acc of anta, end, side).

aṭṭhāsi—sigmatic aor of √ṭhā, to stand, 3rd sing.

ṭhitā—p.p p. fem. of √ṭhā, agreeing with devatā.

sā—pron. used as demonstrative, *that*, fem. qualifying *devatā*.

gāthāya—inst. of gāthā, *f. sing.* √gā, to sing.

ajjhabhāsi—aor. sing 3rd of adhi+abhāsi (a, *augment*+√bhās+i).

Lesson XXX.

PROSODY.

Of all the metres in Pali one that is most commonly used in the Vatta measure. To understand it, the student should know first that—

(*a*) the short vowels are a, i, u

(*b*) the long vowels are ā, ī, ū, e, o

(*c*) the vowel before ṁ is long

(*d*) the vowel before a double consonant is long

(*e*) a short vowel is shown by ◡ and a long vowel by—

(*f*) for the sake of the metre a short vowel may be lengthened or a long vowel shortened.

THE VATTA STANZA.

This consists of four lines or quarter verses, called *padas.* Each pada has generally eight syllables divided thus

	Free.	1st seat.	2nd seat.	Free.
1st pada ...	⏑/—	⏑/— ⏑/— ⏑/—	⏑/— ⏑/— ⏑/—	⏑/—
2nd „ ...	⏑/—	⏑/— ⏑/— ⏑/—	⏑ — ⏑	⏑/—
3rd „ ...	⏑/—	⏑/— ⏑/— ⏑/—	⏑/— ⏑/— ⏑/—	⏑/—
4th „ ...	⏑/—	⏑/— ⏑/— ⏑/—	⏑ — ⏑	⏑/—

Thus the first and the eighth syllables are free *i.e.*, either short or long. In the first seat in all the padas any foot may be used except (⏑ ⏑ ⏑) or (⏑ ⏑—). In the second seat of the first and the third padas any foot may be used, but in the second seat of the second and the fourth padas only (⏑—⏑) must be used. See diagram, *e.g.*

⏑	— ⏑ —	— — —	⏑
Pa	tiṭṭhape	tvā te sat	thu
⏑	— — ⏑	⏑ — ⏑	—
ni	sinnāsa	nabhūmi	yā
—	⏑ — ⏑	⏑ — —	—
in	danīla	mayaṁ thū	paṁ
⏑	— — —	⏑ — ⏑	⏑
ka	ritvā so	apuja	yi

If we have (⏑— —) in the second seat of both the first

and the third padas, the metre is distinguished as *patthyā-vatta.*

	⏑	– – –	⏑ – –	–
e.g.	Ta	to patthā	ya so sat	thā
	⏑	– – –	⏑ – ⏑	–
	vi	nen to de	vamānu	se
	–	⏑ – –	⏑ – –	⏑
	bo	dhito Phus	samāsam	hi
	⏑	⏑ – –	⏑ – ⏑	–
	na	vame puṇ	ṇamasi	yaṁ

VOCABULARY.

PART I PĀLI—ENGLISH.

A

Aggi (*m.*)—"fire."

Ajja (*adv.*)—"to-day."

Añña (*pronl. adj.*)—"other."

Aṭavī (*f.*)—"forest."

Aṭṭhi (*n.*)—"bone."

Attā (*m.*)—"self."

Antare (*advl. loc.*)—"within."

Amacca (*m.*)—"minister," "officer of state."

Amba (*m.*)—"mango."

Ayaṁ—"this," "he."

Araññaṁ—"forest."

Avidūre (*advl. loc.*)—"not far."

Assa (*m.*)—"horse."

Ahaṁ—"I."

Ā

Āgata (*p.p.p.*)—"come."

Āgacchati—"comes," "arrives." √**gam.**

Ācariya (*m.*)—"teacher."

Ācikkhati—"tells," "intimates." √**khyā.**

Āṇā (*f.*)—"order," "command."

Āpaṇa (*m.*)—"market," "shop."

Āmanteti—"calls," "addresses." √**mant.**

Āruhati—"mounts," "ascends." √**ruh.**

Āroceti—"tells," "intimates." √**ruc.**

Āvāṭa (*m.*)—"pit."

Āsanaṁ—"seat."

Āha—"said." √**ah.**

Āharati—"brings," "fetches." √**har.**

Āharāpeti—"causes to bring," "causes to fetch." √**har.**

Āhara (*m.*)—"food."

I

Icchati—"wishes." √**is.**
Icchā (*f.*)—"wish."
Itthī (*f.*)—"woman."
Idāni (*adv.*)—"now."
Iddhi (*f.*)—"miraculous power."

U

Ugganhāti—"acquires." √**gah**
Ucchu (*m.*)—"sugarcane."
Udāhu (*conj.*)—"or."
Upāya (*m.*)—"means," "way."
Uparājā (*m.*)—"viceroy."
Upasaṅkamati—"approaches. √**kam.**
Uppajjati—"arises," "springs up." √**pad.**
Ubho (*m., f., n.*)—"both."
Usu (*m.* or *f.*)—"arrow."

E

Eka—"one."
Esa (= **eso**)—"he, "this."

O

Otarati—"comes down," "descends." √**tar.**
Oloketi—"looks," "beholds." √**lok.**
Ovadati—"admonishes," "instructs." √**vad.**
Ovāda (*m.*)—"admonition."

K

Kata (*p. p. p.*)—"done." √**kar.**
Katheti—"tells, "relates." √**kath.**
Kappeti—"does." √**kapp.**
Kammam—"work," "deed."
Kātum (*inf*) "to do." √**kar.**
Kāraṇam—"matter," "circumstance," "occurrence."
Kināti—"buys." √**ki.**
Kīlati—"plays." √**kīl.**
Kīlā (*f.*)—"play." "sport."
Kumārī—"princess,"
Kusala—"good," "virtuous.'
Ko—"who," "what?"
Koci—"anyone," "whoever."
Koti (*f.*)—"end," "extremity.
Kuṭṭhi (*m.*)—"leper."

Kh

Khanati—"digs." √**khan.**
Khanti (*f.*)—"patience."
Khettaṁ—"field."

G

Gacchati—"goes." √**gam.**
Gacchāpeti—"causes to go."
Gaṅgā (*f.*) "the Ganges."
Gantuṁ (*inf* of √**gam**)—"to go."
Gantvā (*ger.* of √**gam**)—"having gone."
Gahapati (*m.*)—"householder."
Gaheti—"takes," "seizes." √**gah.**
Gāma (*m*)—"village."
Gilāna—"sick."
Guhā (*f.*)—"cave."
Gona (*m*)—"bullock," "cow."
Gopako (*m.*)—"keeper."
Gopāla—"cowherd."

Gh

Ghaṇṭā (*f.*)—"bell"
Ghora—"dreadful," "fearful."

C

Ca (*conj.*)—"and."
Cāṭi (*f.*)—"pot," "vessel."
Catasso (*f.*), **Cattāri** (*n.*), **Cattāro** (*m.*), **Catu** (*base.*)—"four."
Canda (*m*)—"moon."
Citakā (*f.*)—"funeral pile."
Cintayati, **Cinteti**—"thinks." √**cint.**
Ce (*conj.*)—"if."
Cetiyaṁ—"shrine," "pagoda."
Cora (*m*)—"thief."
Corāpeti—"causes to steal."
Coreti—"steals." √**cur.**

Ch

Chaḍḍeti—"gets rid of," "discards." √**chadd.**
Chinna (*p. p. p.*)—"cut," "severed." √**chid.**

J

Janapadaṁ—"district."

Jānāti—"knows." √**jā**.

Jānāpeti—"causes to know."

Jālā (*f*)—"flame."

Jīvitaṁ—"life."

Jeti—"conquers." √**ji**.

T

Tajjeti—"frightens." √**tajj**.

Taṇḍula (*m.*)—"rice."

Tattha (*adv.*)—"there."

Tathā (*adv.*)—"so," "like that."

Tadā (*adv.*)—"then."

Tayo (*m.*)—"three."

Taruṇa—"fresh," "young."

Tāva (*adv.*)—"till." "then."

Ti (*sign of narration*)—"that," "namely."

Tvaṁ—"thou."

Tiṭṭhati—"stands," "remains," "is, established." √**thā**.

Tīṇi (*n.*)—"three."

Tittaka—"bitter."

Tisso (*f.*)—"three."

Tumhe—"you."

D

Dasa—"ten."

Dasseti—"shows," "points out." √**dis**.

Dāpeti—"causes to give." √**dā**.

Dāraka (*m.*)—"boy."

Dārikā (*f.*)—"girl."

Dāru (*n.*)—"firewood," "firestick."

Dāsī (*f.*)—"female slave," "bondwoman."

Dāsa (*m.*)—"male slave," "bondman."

Disā (*f.*)—"cardinal point."

Disvā (*ger.*)—"having seen." √**dis**.

Dīgha—"long."

Dukkha—"painful."

Dukkhaṁ—"pain," "suffering."

Dūta (*m.*)—"messenger," "emissary."

Devī (*f.*)—"queen."

Deseti—"instructs." √**dis**.

Dvi / **Dve** }—"two."

Dosa—"fault," "hatred."

Dh

Dhanam—" wealth."

Dhanu (*n.*)—" bow."

Dhammaṁ—" law," " truth," " the Scriptures."

Dhītā (*f.*)—"daughter."

Dhenu (*f.*)—" cow."

Dhovati—" washes." √**dhov**

N

Naṃ (= **taṁ**)—" him," "that."

Na (*adv.*)—" not."

Nagaraṁ—" town."

Nadī (*f.*)—" river."

Nāmaṁ—" name."

Nāvā (*f.*)—" boat."

Nāvika (*m.*)—" boatman."

Nidahati—" conceals." √**dhā**.

Nipajjati — " lies down." √**pad**.

Nivesanaṁ—"abode," "dwelling."

Nisīdati—" sits. √**sad**.

Nu (*interrogative particle*)—" is it?" " so?"

Neti — " leads," " takes," " brings." √**nī**.

P

Pakkamati—" goes off," " departs." √**kam**.

Pakkosati—" calls," " summons." √**kus**.

Pacati—" cooks." √**pac**.

Pacāmitta (*m.*)—" enemy."

Pacita (*p. p. p.*)—" cooked."

Paccarī (*f.*) ' raft."

Pacchato (*adv.* and *prep.*)— " after," " behind."

Pacchi (*f.*)—" basket."

Pañha (*m.*)—" question."

Pandita (*m.*) — " Pandit," " Sage."

Pandita (*adj.*) — " wise," " clever."

Patvā (*ger.*)—"having attained," " having reached." √**ap**.

Padesa (*m.*) —" place." " spot."

Pana (*conj.*)—" but."

Parājita (*p. p. p.*) — " conquered."

Parājeti—" conquers. √**ji**.

Pavisati—" enters. √**vis**.

Pasu (*m.*)—" goat."

Passati—" sees " √**paṣ**.

Paharita (*p. p. p.*)—" struck."

Paharati—" strikes. √**har**.

Pahinati—"sends." √**hi**.

Pātarāsa (*m.*)—"breakfast."

Pānīyaṁ—"water."

Pāpa—"evil," "wicked."

Pāpuṇāti—"gets," "attains," "reaches" √**ap.**

Pāraṁ (*adv.*, *prep.*, and *noun*)—"beyond."

Pāsāṇa (*m.*)—"rock."

Pāsāda (*m.*)—"palace."

Pitā (*m.*)—"father."

Pitu (*gen.*, *dat.*, and *base* of **pita**)—"father's," etc.

Pidahati—"closes," "shuts." √**dhā.**

Pivati—"drinks." √**pā.**

Pīti (*f.*)—"joy."

Pucchati—"asks." √**pucch**

Putta (*m.*)—"son."

Purato (*adv.* and *prep.*)—"in front."

Purāṇa—"old," "ancient."

Purisa (*m.*)—"man."

Purohita (*m.*)—"private chaplain," "a king's private adviser."

Pesita (*p. p. p.*)—"sent."

Pesati—"sends." √**is.**

Potthaka (*m.* or *n.*)—"book," "treatise."

Ph

Pharusa—"harsh."

Phalaṁ—"fruit"

B

Bandhati—"ties." √**bandh.**

Bahu—"many," "much."

Bārāṇasī (*f.*)—"Benares."

Bāla (*adj.*)—"foolish."

Bālatā (*f.*)—"folly."

Buddha (*m.*)—"Buddha."

Brāhmaṇa (*m.*)—"Brāhmin."

Brāhmaṇī (*f.*)—"Brāhmin's wife."

Bh

Bhaginī (*f.*)—"sister."

Bhaṇḍaṁ—"goods," "property."

Bhaṇḍikā (*f.*)—"bundle."

Bhattaṁ—"rice."

Bhattakāra (*m.*)—"cook."

Bhattā (*m.*)—"husband."

Bhavati—"is." √**bhū.**

Bhātā (*m.*)—"brother."

Bālisika (*m.*)—"fisherman."

Bāhire (*adv.*)—"outside."

Bhikkhavo (*pl.* of **bhikkhu**)—"monks."

Bhikkhu (*m.*)—"monk."

Bhikkunī (*f.*)—"nun."

Bhisi (*f.*)—"mat."

Bhuñjati—"eats." √**bhuj.**

Bhuñjāpeti—"causes to eat."

Bhūmi (*f.*)—"earth."

Bheri (*f.*)—"drum."

Bhojeti—"feeds." √**bhuj.**

M

Magga (*m.*)—"road"

Majjhaṁ—"middle."

Mañcaka (*m.*)—"bed," "cot."

Maṇi (*m.*)—"ruby," "gem."

Madhura—"sweet"

Manussa (*m.*)—"man."

Maṁsaṁ—"flesh."

Mayaṁ—"we."

Maraṇaṁ—"death."

Marati—"dies." √**mar.**

Mahanta—"large," "big."

Mahā (*indecl.*)—"great."

Mahārājā—"emperor," "overlord."

Mā (*prohibitive particle*)—"not."

Mātāpitā—"parents."

Mātā—"mother."

Māreti—"kills." √**mar** (caus.)

Mukhaṁ—"mouth," "face," "entrance."

Mettā (*f.*)—"friendship," "love."

Moceti—"sets free," "releases." √**muc** (caus.)

Y

Yathā (*adv.*)—"as."

Yathāsukhaṁ (*adv. comp.*)—"according to one's wish," "at pleasure."

Yadā (*adv.*)—"when."

Yāva (*adv.*)—"until."

Yāgu (*m.*)—"rice gruel," "porridge."

Yācati—"asks." √**yāc**

Yāti—"goes." √**yā.**

Yogi (*m.*)—"ascetic."

R

Rakkhati—"keeps," "guards." √**rakkh.**

Rajju (*f.*)—"rope," "string."

Raṭṭhaṁ—"kingdom."

Ratti (*f.*)—"night."

Ratha (*m.*)—"chariot," "carriage."

Rasa (*m.*)—"juice."

Rājā (*m.*)—"king"

Rāma (*m.*)—"Rāma."

Rāsi (*m.*)—"heap."

Rukkha (*m.*)—"tree."

L

Labhati—"gets." √**labh**

Lāpu (*n.*)—"pumpkin."

Līḷhā (*f.*)—"grace."

Ludda (*m.*)—"hunter."

V

Vacanaṁ—"speech," "word."

Vañceti—"deceives," "eludes." √**vañc**.

Vā (*conj.*)—"or."

Vādeti—"sounds." √**vad** (*caus*)

Vāreti—"restrains," "checks." √**var**.

Vāsa (*m.*)—"residence."

Vaṭṭati—"is right"

Vaḍḍhaki (*m.*)—"carpenter."

Vatthu (*n*)—"story."

Vadati—"says," "tells." √**vad**

Vadhati—"kills." √**vadh**.

Vasati—"dwells." √**vas**.

Vasāpeti—"causes to dwell."

Vassa—"year."

Vikkiṇāti—"sells." √**ki**.

Vijahati—"forsakes," "abandons." √**hā**;

Vinā (*prep.*)—"without."

Viriyaṁ—"energy."

Vejja (*m*)—"physician," "doctor."

Vīthi (*f.*)—"street," "road."

Vedanaṁ—"pain."

Veḷu (*m.*)—"bamboo."

S

Sakaṭaṁ—"cart."

Sakkā—"able."

Sakuṇa (*m.*)—"bird."

Sakkuṇāti } —"is able." √**sak**.
Sakkoti }

Saccaṁ—"truth."

Sacca—"truthful."

Sace (*conj*)—"if."

Sanna (*f.*)—"sign," "intimation."

Satti (*f.*)—"spear," "javelin."

Saddāhati—"believes." √**dhā**.

Saddhiṁ (*prep*)—"with."

Santikaṁ (*advl. acc*)—"near."

Santike (*adv. loc.*)—"near."

Sabba (*pronl. adj.*)—"all."

Samaya (*m.*)—"time."

Samīpe (*advl. loc.*)—"near.

Sara (*m.*)—"lake."

Sve (*adv.*)—"to-morrow."

S

Sahāya (*m.*)—"friend."

Sā (*f.*)—"she."

Sāṭakaṁ—"garment."

Sāya (*m.*)—"evening."

Sāyaṇha (*m.*)—"evening."

Sāyabhattaṁ—"dinner," "evening meal."

Sārathi (*m.*)—"charioteer."

Sālā (*f.*)—"hall," "room," "rest-house."

Sāsanaṁ—"order," "command," "Buddha's religion."

Sikkhati—"learns." √**sikkh**

Sikkhāpeti—"causes to learn"

Sigāla (*m.*)—"jackal."

Siddhi (*f.*)—"success," "prosperity."

Siri (*f.*)—"glory," "grandeur," "magnificence."

Sissa (*m.*)—"pupil."

Sītala—"cold" "cool."

Sīlaṁ—"precept."

Sīha (*m.*)—"lion."

Sukhaṁ—"happiness."

Suṇāti—"hears," "listens." √**su.**

Suriya (*m.*)—"sun."

Seṭṭhi / **Seṭṭhī** (*m.*)—"banker," "treasurer."

Setu (*m.*)—"bridge."

Senā (*f.*)—"army."

So—"he."

Soḷasa—"sixteen."

H

Hattha (*m.*)—"hand."

Hatthī (*m.*)—"elephant."

Hutvā (*ger.*)—"being." √**hū.**

Heṭṭhā (*adv.* and *prep.*)—"under."

Hoti—"is." √**hū**

—:o:—

Part II. English—Pāli.

A

Able—"**sakkā**."

Abstains—"**viramati**."

According—"**yathā**."

Acquires—"**pāpuṇāti**," "**uggaṇhāti**."

Acts—"**karoti**."

Admonishes—"**ovadati**."

Admonition—"**ovādo**."

Aged—"**mahallaka**."

All—"**sabba**."

Allows—"**labhati.**"

And—"**ca.**"

Another—"**añña.**"

Anyone—"**koci.**"

Approaches—"**upasaṅkamati.**"

Arrives—"**āgacchati.**"

As—"**yathā.**"

Asks—"**pucchati.**"

Assembly—"**parisā.**"

Assents—"**patisuṇāti.**"

Attains—"**pāpuṇāti.**"

B

Be—"**√bhū.**"

Beard—"**massu.**"

Beats—"**paharati.**"

Behind—"**pacchato.**"

Believes—"**saddahati.**"

Bell—"**ghaṇṭā.**"

Bhagavā—"**Bhagavā.**"

Bird—"**sakuṇo.**"

Birth—"**jāti.**"

Boat—"**nāvā.**"

Book—"**potthakaṁ.**"

Both—"**ubho.**"

Boy—"**dārako.**"

Brahmin—"**Brāhmaṇo.**"

Breakfast—"**pātarāso.**"

Brings—"**āharati.**"

Brother—"**bhātā.**"

Brought—"**āharita,**" "**ānīta.**"

Buddha—"**Buddha.**"

Bullock—"**goṇo.**"

C

Calls—"**pakkosati.**"

Can—"**sakkā**" "**sakkoti,**" "**sakkuṇāti.**"

Cardinal Point—"**disā.**"

Carpenter—"**vaḍḍhaki.**"

Cart—"**sakaṭaṁ.**"

Cause—"**kāraṇaṁ.**"

Chaplain (private)—"**purohito.**"

Chariot—"**ratho.**"

Charioteer—"**sārathi.**"

Checks—"**vāreti.**"

City—"**nagaraṁ.**"

Clever—"**paṇḍita.**"

Comes—"**āgacchati.**"

Commits—"**karoti.**"

Company—"**parisā.**"

Compass (point of)—"**disā.**"

Conceals—"**nidahati.**"

Conversation—"**kathā.**"

Cooks—"**pacati.**"

Cow—"**dhenu.**"

Cowherd—"**gopālo.**"

Creeper—"**valli.**"

D

Dares—"**ussahati**."
Daughter—"**dhītā**."
Day—"**divaso**."
Death—"**maraṇaṁ**."
Deceives—"**vañceti**."
Declares—"**katheti**," "**ārocceti**."
Deed—"**kammaṁ**."
Departs—"**pakkamati**."
Descends—"**otarati**."
Describes—"**vaṇṇeti**."
Destroys—"**nāseti**."
Did—"**akāsi**."
Dies—"**marati**."
Digs—"**khanati**"
Direction—"**disā**."
Divides—"**bhājeti**."
Doctor—"**vejjo**."
Does—"**karoti**."
Done (*p. p. p.*)—"**kata**."
Door—"**dvāraṁ**."
Dreadful—"**ghora**."
Drinks—"**pivati**."
Drum—"**bheri**."
Dwelling—"**nivesanaṁ**."
Dwells—"**vasati**," "**viharati**."

E

Eats—"**khādati**," "**bhuñjati**."
Eight—"**aṭṭha**."
Eighty—"**asīti**."
Elephant—"**hatthī**"
Emissary—"**dūto**."
Emperor—"**mahārājā**."
Endeavours—"**ussahati**."
Enmity—"**veraṁ**."
Enters—"**pavisati**."
Evening—"**sāyaṇho**."
Evil—"**pāpaṁ**."
Excavation—"**āvāṭo**."
Exertion—"**viriyaṁ**."
Eye—"**cakkhu**."

F

Falls—"**patati**."
Far—"**dūre**," "**dūrato**."
Father—"**pitā**."
Fault—"**doso**."
Fear—"**bhayaṁ**."
Feeds—"**bhojeti**."
Field—"**khettaṁ**."
Firewood—"**dāru**."
First—"**paṭhama**."
Fisherman—"**bāḷisiko**."
Five—"**pañca**."
Folly—"**bālatā**."
Foolish—"**bāla**."
Foot—"**pādo**."

Foot-soldier—"**patti.**"
Four—"**catu.**"
Fourth—"**catuttha.**"
Friend—"**sahāyo.**"
Frightens—"**tajjeti.**"
Front (*m.*)—"**purato.**"

G

Garden—"**uyyanāṁ.**"
Garment—"**sāṭakaṁ.**"
Gets—"**labhati,**" "**gaṇhāti.**"
Gets rid—"**chaḍḍeti.**"
Gift—"**dānaṁ.**"
Girl—"**dārikā.**"
Gives—"**dadāti;**" "**deti.**"
Glory—"**siri,**" "**sirī.**"
God—"**devo.**"
Goes—"**gacchati.**"
Gold—"**suvaṇṇaṁ.**"
Goods—"**bhaṇḍaṁ,**" "**bhaṇḍāni.**"
Grandson—"**nattā.**"
Great—"**mahā,**" "**mahanta.**"

H

Hall—"**sālā.**"
Hand—"**hattho.**"
Happiness—"**sukhaṁ.**"
Harp—"**tantī.**"
He—"**so.**"
He who—"**yo.**"
Hears—"**suṇāti.**"
Here—"**idha.**"
High—"**ucca.**"
Hire—"**bhati.**"
Hole—"**āvāṭa.**"
Honey—"**madhu.**"
Honour—"**sakkāro**"
Horse—"**asso.**"
Hot—"**uṇha.**"
House—"**gharaṁ.**"
Hundred—"**sataṁ.**"
Hunter—"**luddo.**"

I

I—"**ahaṁ.**"
If—"**ce,**" "**sace.**"
Impossible—"**na sakkā;**" "**na sakkoti,**" "**na sakkuṇāti.**"
Is—"**hoti.**"
Is able—"**sakkuṇāti;**" "**sakkā,**" "**sakkoti.**"

J

Javelin..."**satti.**"

K

Keeps—"**rakkhati.**"
Killed—"**mārita.**"
Kills—"**māreti.**"
King—"**rājā.**"

L

Law—"**dhammo.**"
Learns—"**sikkhati.**"
Life—"**jīvitam.**"
Lion—"**sīho.**"
Lioness—"**sīhī.**"
Listens—"**suṇāti.**"
Lives—"**vasati,**" "**viharati.**"
Long—"**dīgha.**"
Looks—"**oloketi.**"
Lute—"**vīṇā.**"

M

Magnificence—"**siri,**" "**sirī.**"
Makes—"**karoti,**" "**kappeti.**"
Man—"**puriso,**" "**manusso.**"
Many—"**bahu.**"
Matter—"**pavatti,**" "**kāraṇam.**"
Means—"**upāyo.**"
Medicine—"**osadham.**"
Merchant—"**vāṇijo.**"
Messenger—"**dūto.**"
Middle—"**majjham.**"
Minister—"**amacco.**"
Monastery—"**vihāro.**"
Monk—"**bhikkhu,**" "**samano.**"
Monkey—"**kapi,**" **vānaro.**"
Moon—"**cando.**"
Mother—"**mātā.**"
Mountain—"**pabbato.**"

N

Name—"**nāmam.**"
Names—"**nāmam karoti.**"
New—"**nava.**"
Near—"**antike,**" "**samīpe.**"
Nineteen..."**ekūnavīsati.**"
Not—"**na,**" "**mā.**"
Not far—"**avidūre.**"
Now—"**idāni.**"
Nun—"**bhikkhunī.**"

O

Old—"**purāṇa.**"
One—"**eka.**"
Or—"**vā.**" "**udāhu.**"
Other—"**añña.**"
Outside—"**bāhire.**"

P

Pain—"**vedanā.**"
Painful—"**dukkha.**"
Pagoda—"**cetiyaṁ.**"
Palace—"**pāsādo.**"
Pandit—"**paṇḍito.**"
Parents—"**mātapitā.**"
Park—"**uyyānaṁ.**"
Patience—"**khanti.**"
People—"**mahājano;**" "**purisā,**" "**manussā.**"
Person—"**puriso,**" "**manusso.**"
Physician—"**vejjo.**"
Pit—"**āvāṭo.**"
Place—"**ṭhānaṁ.**"
Plan—"**upāyo.**"
Pleasure—"**rati.**"
Point (of the compass)—"**disā.**"
Precept—"**sīlaṁ.**"
Presence (of)—"**santike.**"
Property—"**bhaṇḍaṁ.**"
Pride—"**mano.**"
Proud—"**mana.**"
Pumpkin—"**lāpu.**"
Pupil—"**sisso,**" "**sāvako,**" "**antevāsiko.**"

Q

Queen—"**devī.**"
Question—"**pañho.**"

R

Reaches—"**pāpuṇāti.**"
Reason—"**kāraṇaṁ.**"
Receives—"**labhati.**"
Rejoices—"**modati.**"
Relic—"**dhātu,**"
Religion—"**dhammo.**"
Remembers—"**sarati.**"
Removes—"**apaneti.**"
Resident-pupil—"**antivāsiko.**"
Restrains—"**vāreti.**"
Retinue—"**parisa.**"
Rice—"**bhattaṁ.**"
Rice-gruel—"**yāgu.**"
Rids—"**chaḍḍeti.**"
Right (it is)—"**vaṭṭati.**"
Rings—"**vādeti.**"
River—"**nadī.**"
Road—"**vīthi.**"
Robber—"**coro.**"
Rock—"**pāsāṇo.**"
Room—"**okāsa,**" "**ṭhānaṁ,**" "**sālā.**"

S

Sailor—"**nāviko.**"
Sand—"**vālukā.**"
Says—"**katheti,**" "**vadati.**"
Science—"**sippaṁ.**"

Second—" **dutiya.**"
Seated (*p.p.p.*)—" **nisinna.**"
Sees—" **passati,**" " **oloketi.**"
Sells—" **vikkiṇāti.**"
Sends—" **peseti.**"
Seven—" **satta.**"
Share—**koṭṭhāsa.**"
She—" **sā.**"
Shop—**āpaṇo.**"
Shows—" **dasseti.**"
Sick—" **gilāna.**"
Sister—" **bhaginī.**"
Sits—" **nisīdati.**"
Sky—" **ākāso.**"
Slave—" **dāso.**"
Slave-woman—" **dāsī.**"
So—" **tathā,**" " **evaṁ.**"
Soldier—" **yodho.**"
Son—" **putto.**"
Sounds—" **vādeti.**"
Spade—" **kuddālo.**"
Speaks—" **katheti.**"
Spear—" **satti.**"
Stands—" **ṭhāti,**" **tiṭṭhāti.**"
Star—" **tārakā.**"
Stays—" **vasati,**" " **viharati.**
Steals—" **coreti.**"
Story—" **vatthu.**"
Street—" **vīthi.**"
String—" **rajju.**"
Success—" **siddhi.**"
Suffering—" **dukkhaṁ.**"
Suffers (death)—" **maraṇaṁ pāpuṇāti.**"
Sugar-cane—" **ucchu.**"
Sun—" **suriyo.**"
Supports—" **poseti.**"

T

Takes—" **gaṇheti,**" " **gaṇhāti.**"
Teacher—" **satthā,**" " **ācariyo.**"
Teaches—" **sikkhati,**" " **upadisati.**"
Tear—" **assu.**"
Tells—" **āroceti,**" " **katheti.**"
There—" **tattha.**"
Thief—" **coro.**"
Thinks—" **cinteti.**"
This—" **eso.**"
Thorn—" **kaṇṭako.**"
Thousand—" **sahassaṁ.**"
Thou—" **tvaṁ.**"
Three—" **ti.**"
Throws—" **khipati.**"
Throws up—" **ukkhipati.**"
Thunderbolt—" **asanī.**"
Thy—" **tava,**" " **te,**" " **tuyhaṁ.**"
Ties—" **bandhati.**"
Till then—" **tāva,**" " **tāvatā.**"

To-day—"**ajja.**"
To-morrow—"**sve.**"
Top—"**matthako.**"
Town—"**nagaraṁ**"
Townsman—"**nagara vāsī.**
Treasure—"**dhanaṁ.**"
Truth—"**saccaṁ.**"
Two—"**dvi.**"

U

Uncle—"**mātulo.**"
Under—"**heṭṭhā,**" "(**indcl.**)."
Understands—"**parijānāti.**
Until—"**tāva.**"

V

Various—"**vividha.**"
Viceroy—"**uparāja.**"
Victory—"**vijayo.**"
Village—"**gāmo.**"
Virtue—"**guṇo.**

W

Wanders—"**pāriyāyati.**"
War—**yuddhaṁ.**"
Washes—"**dhovati.**"
Water—"**pānīyaṁ.**"
We—"**mayaṁ.**"
Wealth—"**dhanaṁ.**"
Weapon—"**āvudhaṁ.**"
Well (very)—"**sādhu.**"
Went—"**agamāsi.**"
What—"**yo,**" "**ko.**"
When—"**yadā,**" "**kadā.**"
Where—"**yattha,**" "**kattha.**"
Which }—"**yo,**" "**ko.**"
Who }
Why—"**kiṁ.**"
Wicked—"**pāpa.**"
Wisdom—"**paññā.**"
Wise—"**paṇḍita.**"
Wish—"**icchā.**"
Wishes—"**icchati.**"
Within—"**antare.**"
Without—"**vinā,**" "**bāhire.**
Woman—"**itthī.**"
Word—"**vācā.**"
Work—"**kammaṁ.**"
World—"**loko.**"

Y

Year—"**saṁvaccharo.**"
Yes—"**āma.**"
Yesterday—"**hīyo,**" (*ir. dcl.*)
You—"**tumhe.**"
Young—"**taruṇa.**" "**dahara.**"